Social-Historical Readings of Literary, Theological, and Narrative Themes and Motifs in Luke-Acts

Social-Historical Readings of Literary, Theological, and Narrative Themes and Motifs in Luke-Acts

Michael Blythe

WIPF & STOCK · Eugene, Oregon

SOCIAL-HISTORICAL READINGS OF LITERARY, THEOLOGICAL, AND NARRATIVE THEMES AND MOTIFS IN LUKE-ACTS

Copyright © 2024 Michael Blythe. All rights reserved. Except for brief quotations in critical publications or reviews, no part of this book may be reproduced in any manner without prior written permission from the publisher. Write: Permissions, Wipf and Stock Publishers, 199 W. 8th Ave., Suite 3, Eugene, OR 97401.

Wipf & Stock
An Imprint of Wipf and Stock Publishers
199 W. 8th Ave., Suite 3
Eugene, OR 97401

www.wipfandstock.com

PAPERBACK ISBN: 979-8-3852-1175-3
HARDCOVER ISBN: 979-8-3852-1176-0
EBOOK ISBN: 979-8-3852-1177-7

VERSION NUMBER 06/27/24

Unless otherwise noted, Scripture quotations are from the New English Translation (NET). Scripture quoted by permission. NET Bible® copyright ©1996, 2019 by Biblical Studies Press, L.L.C. http://netbible.com All rights reserved.

Scripture quotations marked (NIV) are taken from the Holy Bible, New International Version®, NIV®. Copyright © 1973, 1978, 1984, 2011 by Biblica, Inc.® Used by permission of Zondervan. All rights reserved worldwide. www.zondervan.com The "NIV" and "New International Version" are trademarks registered in the United States Patent and Trademark Office by Biblica, Inc.®

Scripture quotations marked (NRSV) are taken from the New Revised Standard Version Bible, copyright © 1989, Division of Christian Education of the National Council of the Churches of Christ in the United States of America. Used by permission. All rights reserved.

Scripture quotations marked (BfE) are reproduced from The Bible for Everyone, copyright © John Goldingay and Nicholas Thomas Wright 2018. Used by permission of the Society for Promoting Christian Knowledge, London, UK. All rights reserved.

This work is dedicated to my mother, Alice, for the love, sacrifice, and opportunities she has given me; without her investment, my course in life would be drastically different.

Contents

Preface | ix
Acknowledgments | xi
Abbreviations | xii
Introduction | xiii

Chapter 1: The Good Samaritan in Social-Scientific Perspective | 1

Chapter 2: A Social-Scientific Reading of Zechariah's Status Reversal in Luke 1:5–25 | 12

Chapter 3: The Progression of Controversy and Response in Mark 1:21—3:6 with Implications for Lukan Redaction | 27

Chapter 4: A Galilean Peasant's Reception: "The Prodigal Son" in the Context of Luke's Travel Narrative, a Social-Scientific Reading | 40

Chapter 5: A Social-Scientific Analysis of Simon the Magician's Request in Acts 8 | 48

Chapter 6: Election and Divine Sovereignty in Acts 8:26—10:48 in Relation to the Gentile Mission | 60

Chapter 7: Luke's Progressive Revelation of Jesus's Identity—Son of God, King, and Christ | 68

Chapter 8: Deuteronomic History and the Portrayal of Solomon in Luke-Acts | 76

Chapter 9: Ears and Heart Circumcision in Luke-Acts | 86

Chapter 10: Father, Son, and Spirit: Symbols of Patronage and Reciprocity in Luke-Acts | 97

Chapter 11: Inspired Meals in Luke-Acts: Food and Table Fellowship as a Means of Grace | 112

CONTENTS

Chapter 12: The Gospel Message of Acts: The Good News to the Ends of the Earth | 128

Chapter 13: Where's the Love? An Exploration of the Infrequent Theme in Luke-Acts | 154

Bibliography | 169

Preface

My academic work across multiple masters' degrees and subsequent doctoral work in the most recent six years has near exclusively focused on Luke-Acts. Moreover, I have enjoyed the opportunity in both academic and parish settings to teach through Luke and Acts various times in recent years. From my scholarly engagement I have been able to give limited attention to diverse research areas in Lukan scholarship that merit expansion.

This volume is an accumulation of thirteen individual Luke-Acts research efforts, many with a unique viewpoint on Acts. The chapters include presentations (with adaptations) made at various conferences from 2021 to 2024, including the Society of Biblical Literature, British New Testament Society, Wesleyan Theological Society, and Evangelical Theological Society. Other essay selections come from research colloquium presentations at Africa Nazarene University (Nairobi, Kenya), and academic work researched while studying at Reformed Theological Seminary (Jackson, Mississippi). Many of the chapters within this volume include material that has been heretofore largely unexplored in Luke-Acts, offering fertile ground for further exploration by future scholarship. Other chapters discuss topics that have been well-treated within Luke-Acts, but which remain ripe for ongoing academic dialogue.

My scholarly discipline tends to be eclectic, often employing a social-scientific methodology, which blends sociological and cultural anthropological theories with social and historical assessments of the world behind the text. In most of these chapters, social-scientific criticism is a bedrock of the work. However, I also gravitate to various literary and narrative components in the Lukan writings, which in some of these chapters complements the socio-historical research, while a few other chapters rely solely on narrative and thematic development.

Acknowledgments

FIRST AND FOREMOST, I express thankfulness to my family, specifically my household, who, since the beginning, have been sacrificially supportive of my scholarly journey, especially my wife, Kristen, who eagerly and lovingly assists my endeavors.

Next, I am grateful for my ecclesial community, particularly Salem United Methodist Church and Shiloh United Methodist Church, who have enabled my progression into scholarship for these last seven years, and more recently Centenary United Methodist Church, each of which I currently pastor in Mecklenburg County, Virginia. Moreover, the mid-week Bible study group at First Baptist Church (Chase City, Virginia) where I have now taught for three years is also a vital part of my faith connection. Additionally, I offer appreciation to the Rev. James (Jay) Carey, my episcopal supervisor, whose trust is humbling, and his confidence has empowered me to be the best version of myself as a pastor and disciple.

Last but not least, I am blessed with the encouragement and affirmation of the academic community surrounding me, including Rev. Dr. Tom Cribb, instrumental in igniting my passion for biblical studies; Rev. Charles (Chuck) Crocker (PhD candidate), who supplies ongoing intellectually stimulating conversation; Rev. Dr. Dan Woods, a daily encourager and confidence builder; and the collective of Africa Nazarene University, whose faculty has sown into my growing scholarship.

Abbreviations

BfE	*The Bible for Everyone*
BrillDAG	*The Brill Dictionary of Ancient Greek*
HTS	*Hervormde Teologiese Studies*
IVP	Intervarsity Press
NET	New English Translation
NIDNTTE	*New International Dictionary of New Testament Theology and Exegesis*
NIV	New International Version
NRSV	New Revised Standard Version
TDNT	*Theological Dictionary of the New Testament*

Introduction

EACH OF THESE THIRTEEN selections are designed as distinct topics. However, there is extensive overlap among the content in many chapters, especially regarding social-scientific criticism, in addition to the intersection of various literary themes and motifs. Therefore, to those whose interest might be limited to an individual portion but who seek a better understanding of the methodological basis, it may be helpful to consult various chapters within this volume.

Chapter 1, "The Good Samaritan in Social-Scientific Perspective," begins with a brief explanation of social-scientific criticism and uses this parable to example how the methodology may be applied. (This parable is thoroughly discussed in *The Priest and Levite as Temple Representatives*, published in 2023 by Wipf & Stock.) This chapter enhances the typical reading of this well-known parable by incorporating social, historical, economic, literary, and anthropological factors, beginning by first applying these methods to the parable itself, then situating the findings to the broader Lukan narratives.

Chapter 2, "A Social-Scientific Reading of Zechariah's Status Reversal in Luke 1:5–25," offers a re-examination of this Lukan passage with new eyes. This chapter generates a unique reading of Luke's introductory narrative, especially the perceptions regarding Zechariah, using social-scientific criticism, but also expands the reading by employing literary and theological components wherein status reversal, a hallmark of Lukan theology, is initially conveyed via the male, honorable, priest being shamed, while his infertile wife is elevated.

Chapter 3, "The Progression of Controversy and Response in Mark 1:21—3:6 with Implications for Lukan Redaction," begins by noting the existing but limited work remarking on literary elements within these passages. This chapter then expands upon these resources to highlight how Mark constructed his sequence in a way of steadily progressing Jesus's controversies early in his Galilean ministry, likely motivating Luke's retention of this order within his Gospel in Luke 5:12—6:11 as he prioritized the marginalized categories highlighted by this escalation.

Chapter 4, "A Galilean Peasant's Reception: 'The Prodigal Son' in the Context of Luke's Travel Narrative, a Social-Scientific Reading," leans heavily on Kenneth Bailey and Richard Rohrbaugh's assessment of this parable, but it furthers the conversation primarily by considering the reception of this story from a first-century peasant's perspective. This generates an understanding of how the story was designed to deliver a greater offense than what is typically recognized, potentially alienating Jesus from his strongest audience constituency. Moreover, this chapter opens the door to further literary connection to the broader context of Luke's travel narrative.

Chapter 5, "A Social-Scientific Analysis of Simon the Magician's Request in Acts 8," utilizes social background to render a robust and unique reading of this narrative, drawing on essential factors of first century Mediterranean and Palestinian life, especially the concepts of patronage, honor, and shame, providing a greater understanding of a complicated passage.

Chapter 6, "Election and Divine Sovereignty in Acts 8:26—10:48 in Relation to the Gentile Mission," offers less of a contribution and more of an assessment likely shared by other works of scholarship. However, this section raises further research questions prudent for academic exploration. It considers the triple encounter near the turning point of Acts with the Ethiopian eunuch, Saul/Paul of Tarsus, and Cornelius and how these unique narratives shape the expansion of missionary activities in Acts.

Chapter 7, "Luke's Progressive Revelation of Jesus's Identity—Son of God, King, and Christ," shifts to examining Luke-Acts as a whole, rather than just a singular passage. This chapter highlights a key literary function that scholars have partly observed, but it contributes by considering the various ways Luke unfolds key ascriptions to Jesus, often being initially attested by God, angels, and unclean spirits followed by nuanced human affirmation. This chapter concludes by noting further prospects for ongoing scholarly dialogue.

Chapter 8, "Deuteronomic History and the Portrayal of Solomon in Luke-Acts," contributes by establishing a subject matter that scholarship otherwise ignores. Employing narrative and literary observations with historical considerations from the Old Testament in combination with Lukan theology, this chapter generates a unique engagement that is open to further expansion, arguing that Luke-Acts depicts Solomon suspiciously at best, and negatively at worst, due to Luke's emphasis on material ethics and new temple theology.

Chapter 9, "Ears and Heart Circumcision in Luke-Acts," begins with Stephen's assertion in Acts 7, in which he states, "'You stubborn people, with uncircumcised hearts and ears!'" This chapter traces the literary progression of each named concept—ears, heart, and circumcision—through the Old Testament and then the whole of Luke-Acts, discussing how each aspect connects to circumcision, becoming a critical variable as Luke highlights missionary activity among the gentile nations.

Chapter 10, "Father, Son, and Spirit: Symbols of Patronage and Reciprocity in Luke-Acts," is broad in scope, incorporating all of Luke-Acts, and presents key dynamics of the collectivistic social world of the Bible. This chapter expands upon the very brief and limited works of other scholars by incorporating the role of the Holy Spirit into the patronage model, significantly, as the currency exchange between God the patron, and his client church. This chapter asserts many historical, literary, narrative features with implications to provide a theological reading for Lukan pneumatology.

Chapter 11, "Inspired Meals in Luke-Acts: Food and Table Fellowship as a Means of Grace," explores the relationship between grace and table fellowship within the Lukan corpus, a fascinating concept that is pervasive in the text. This essay establishes ongoing research possibilities regarding how this literary and thematic connection might assist in development within modern practical and liturgical theology.

Chapter 12, "The Gospel Message of Acts: The Good News to the Ends of the Earth," traces the literary and narrative sequences through Acts, examining instances where the gospel material is presented while establishing the Lukan message of salvation emphasizes Jesus's life, death, resurrection, and his ongoing function following the ascension; however, remarkably absent are many individualistic qualities, including the penal rescue from Hell, or even the eternal residence in Heaven.

Chapter 13, "Where's the Love? An Exploration of the Infrequent Theme in Luke-Acts," contributes by treating an ill-explored feature in the Lukan corpus, Luke's usage of "love." The chapter begins by examining and synthesizing each time Luke uses a word normally translated as "love," as well as the literary and narrative relationship of this concept to broader Lukan motifs and theology including socio-economic ethics. A

INTRODUCTION

portion of this contribution is devoted to contending that God demonstrates love in Acts, even while the word is entirely absent from the text of Luke's second volume.

Chapter 1: The Good Samaritan in Social-Scientific Perspective

THIS CHAPTER APPLIES SPECIFIC social-scientific hermeneutical aspects to the parable of the good Samaritan (Luke 10:25–37).[1]

Social-Scientific Criticism Defined

Social-scientific criticism, simply defined, is an analysis of "the social and cultural dimensions of the text and of its environmental context through the utilization of the perspectives, theory, models, and research of the social sciences."[2] To a responsible exegete, attention to this background analysis is an imperative.[3]

At the foundation of this social-scientific process is a recognition that when approaching Scripture, the exegete is prone to impose his or her own socio-cultural assumptions onto the text.[4] Therefore, it is a necessity to recognize the unique qualities that distinguish the Middle Eastern and Mediterranean cultures of the Bible. Accordingly, cultural concepts such as friendship, hospitality, kinship, and patronage are viewed very differently in those cultures than in other parts of the contemporary world.[5] When these vital cultural contexts are ignored, the interpreter will fail to capture

---

1. Presented at Africa Nazarene University School of Religion and Christian Ministry research colloquium on November 6, 2020.
2. Elliott, *What Is Social-Scientific Criticism?*, 7.
3. Fee, *New Testament Exegesis*, 134.
4. Fee, *New Testament Exegesis*, 135.
5. Pilch and Malina, *Handbook of Biblical Social Values*, xix.

significant portions of meaning from the text.⁶ Hence, Richard Rohrbaugh rightly assesses that a "cross-cultural reading of the Bible is not a choice" when it comes to responsible exegesis.⁷

While this methodology was born out of the historical-critical approach originating from the late nineteenth century,⁸ its early association with higher criticism does not negate the benefits of use by modern evangelical traditions even.⁹ One crucial consideration is that socio-cultural findings are not intended to stand alone when drawing conclusions from the text, but rather are a complementary step in the exegetical process.¹⁰

An Introduction to Honor-Shame Culture

In the first-century world of the text, honor and shame were social fundamentals.¹¹ The honor-shame paradigm was an instrument used to reinforce the values of the society.¹² When people complied with acceptable virtues, they would receive a prescribed sense of honor. Alternatively, failure to adhere to the cultural norms resulted in shame.¹³ This not only served to address the infractions of the one crossing those social boundaries, but also created a deterrent against potential anti-social behavior by others.¹⁴

Arriving at a concise definition of honor can be challenging, as there are various types of honor and different means of achievement.¹⁵ First,

6. DeSilva, *Honor, Patronage, Kinship and Purity*, 18–19.
7. Rohrbaugh, *Social Sciences and New Testament Interpretation*, 1.
8. Dvorak, "Elliott's Social-Scientific Criticism," 251–78.
9. Berding, "Hermeneutical Framework," 3–22.
10. Elliott, *Home for the Homeless*, 7–8.
11. DeSilva, *Honor, Patronage, Kinship and Purity*, 22–23. DeSilva identifies words and their derivations that are commonly associated with honor-shame, including "glory," "reputation" (*doxa*), "honor" (*timē*), and "praise" (*epainos*). These, together with verb and adjectival forms, are used frequently in the Bible texts, along with their antonyms, "dishonor" (*aischunē*), "reproach" (*oneidos*), "scorn" (*kataphronēsis*), "slander" (*blasphēmia*).
12. Richards and James, *Misreading Scripture*, 134.
13. Richards and James, *Misreading Scripture*, 175.
14. It can be especially difficult to grasp the first-century social implications of honor and shame for those who live outside these types of societies. For example, northern European societies tend to be guilt-based cultures. A simplistic distinction is that guilt is a more personal trait, which aligns with the individualism of European-based societies, whereas the concept shame takes on a corporate context, which is more intuitive for those from cultures oriented around a community identity.
15. Richards and James, *Misreading Scripture*, 136.

honor as a collective principle is a foundation of community-based societies. Therefore, in honor cultures, matters of ancestry and other social identification maintain a primary role in what is called ascribed honor.[16] With this form of honor, one might be an impoverished peasant, but still have the potential for greater honor than someone with wealth.[17] This is because while the two are correlated, honor itself is considered the higher quality than wealth.[18] An example of ascribed honor is observed in the role of the firstborn son.

An additional method of acquiring honor was through deeds; this is called achieved honor.[19] The more virtuous works accomplished, the more honor would be associated with that person.[20] Jesus was considered to have achieved high marks of honor through instances of healing. Many with specific illness and handicaps were considered impure, with little to no honor. Prior to Jesus's intervention, these individuals were relegated to social exile since first-century Judaism often lacked a clear distinction between ritual and moral impurity.[21] Hence, while Jesus was manufacturing his own honor via healing, he was also reinstituting honor, worth, and dignity to those he healed, by their return to society.[22]

Honor Challenges

One method of enhancing honor status was through public contests called honor challenges. The victor in such occurrences would achieve increased honor, while the unsuccessful counterpart would suffer shame. The judge of the outcome would be the observing spectators. How one responded or elected not to respond was subject to scrutiny. For instance, it would be less likely for a person of higher status to accept a challenge from someone beneath their honor scale. Therefore, most honor challenges took place

---

16. DeSilva, *Honor, Patronage, Kinship and Purity*, 28.
17. Richards and James, *Misreading Scripture*, 138–39.
18. Richards and James, *Misreading Scripture*, 134.
19. DeSilva, *Honor, Patronage, Kinship and Purity*, 28.
20. Richards and James, *Misreading Scripture*, 145–46.
21. Wright and Bird, *New Testament in Its World*, 211. It could also be argued that people in other social categories suffered a form of exile and were impoverished, particularly those who were bankrupt and women.
22. Pilch and Malina, *Handbook of Biblical Social Values*, loc. 89.

between people whose honor status paralleled.[23] The ramifications of an honor challenge were serious, as "one's place in society, one's vocation, the family business, or a child's marriage options all could be at stake."[24]

Honor could be challenged in many ways through a variety of actions or words. Questioning was one instance that would have automatically engaged one in a defense of honor. As Rohrbaugh asserts, in the ancient world of Jesus, "questions are always challenges in public";[25] every human interaction was an opportunity to further implement one's personal honor or be subjected to shame. This amounts to what Pilch calls the "push and shove" game, an essential interaction of that culture.[26] Pilch described these games in the following terms:

> The contest begins with a challenge (almost any word, gesture, action) that seeks to undermine the honor of another person and a response that answers in equal measure or ups the ante (and thereby challenges in return). Both positive (gifts, compliments) and negative challenges (insults, dares) must be answered to avoid a serious loss of face.[27]

This action often included the "art of insult" which was not only considered to be an appropriate response, but also a requirement for any male. Pilch further observes that had Jesus been unable to respond to challenges utilizing this art, none of his contemporaries would have ever taken him seriously.[28] Fortunately for Jesus, he was a master at insult.[29] Such instances of his effective countermeasure to a questioner are observed in his "Have you not read?" responses found throughout the Gospel narratives.[30]

This type of interaction is found at the occasion of the parable of the good Samaritan (Luke 10:25–37) when the lawyer poses the question to Jesus (Luke 10:25). Since no question was innocent in this culture, and this lawyer, being an interpreter of the Torah, was socially comparable to Jesus, a teacher, this question represented an honor challenge that must be defended. Jesus's defense begins by redirecting the question, placing the lawyer on the

23. DeSilva, *Honor, Patronage, Kinship and Purity*, 29.
24. Richards and James, *Misreading Scripture*, 159.
25. Rohrbaugh, *Honor and Shame*, 21:59–22:02.
26. Pilch, *Cultural Handbook to the Bible*, 158.
27. Pilch and Malina, *Handbook of Biblical Social Values*, 93.
28. Pilch, *Cultural Handbook to the Bible*, 162.
29. Rohrbaugh, *Honor and Shame*.
30. Pilch, *Cultural Handbook to the Bible*, 161.

defensive (10:27). However, the lawyer still carries the agenda of an honor challenge and continues the line of questioning (10:29), at which point Jesus responds to the challenge through the lesson in parable.[31] Eventually, Jesus wins the "push and shove" game when the lawyer retreats, having validated the point of the parable through his response to Jesus.

The Jewish Purity System

The Jewish purity system involved distinct levels of status related to honor. John Pilch offers a concise definition and summary of the Jewish purity system in biblical times:

> Purity is a value that directs each member of a society to respect and observe the system of space and timelines that human groups develop to have everything in its place and a place for everything. In Mediterranean biblical society, purity marks a person who knows how to be clean rather than unclean.[32]

Pilch further assesses that purification standards can be violated in four ways.[33] The first of these violations, external threats, occurs when the covenant people were influenced from the outside. Examples of these purity violations include taking foreign wives or idols.[34] The Jewish people viewed Samaritans, whose heritage was comingled with both Jewish and gentile ethnicities, as a first order threat representing the infiltration of outside blood.

The second purity violation came from interior threats. This happened when individuals deviated from their expected roles. For example, the Levitical laws regarding homosexuality fall within this category, as keeping a specific sexual order was expected.[35] In the third violation, the margins of society are threatened when boundaries become penetrable. This encompasses dietary concerns, natural bodily occurrences,[36] and certain

---

31. N. T. Wright renders the seldom-used Greek ὑπολαμβάνω (*hypolambanō*) from Luke 10:30 "Jesus rose to the challenge," which captures the social dimension of this dialogue. See Wright's Bible translation, *Bible for Everyone* (BfE), on copyright page of this volume.
32. Pilch and Malina, *Handbook of Biblical Social Values*, 147.
33. Pilch and Malina, *Handbook of Biblical Social Values*, 147.
34. Pilch and Malina, *Handbook of Biblical Social Values*, 147.
35. Pilch and Malina, *Handbook of Biblical Social Values*, 147.
36. For example, childbirth and genital discharge.

illnesses.[37] Finally, the fourth violation is contradictory or inconsistent behavior within a group.[38] Jesus exposed examples of this behavior, perhaps most notably when he addressed the hypocrisy of the Pharisees.

Within Jewish life, purity was categorized according to space, time, and class. What subsequently developed was a linear purity map. Note the Ten Degrees of Holiness from the Mishnaic Tradition[39] to illustrate how categories of space were organized in the following way:

> The land of Israel is holier than any other land.
> The walled cities [of the land of Israel] are holier still . . .
> Within the walls of Jerusalem is still more holy . . .
> The Temple Mount is still more holy . . .
> The Rampart [surrounding the Temple precincts] is still more holy . . .
> The Court of the Women is still more holy . . .
> The Court of the Israelites is still more holy . . .
> The Court of the Priests is still more holy . . .
> Between the Porch and the Altar is still more holy . . .
> The sanctuary [the holy place] is still more holy . . .
> And the Holy of Holies is still more holy . . . .[40]

In this depiction, geography is made clear, that the closer one is to the temple, the more holy the ground. Likewise, in contrast, the further one is from the temple, the less sacred the ground.

To further describe the first-century view of individual purity, there is tradition found in the Tosefta Megilla in the following purity map regarding people:

1. Priests

2. Levites

3. Israelites

4. Converts (proselytes)

5. Freed slaves

---

37. Skin sores would be a common example.

38. Pilch and Malina, *Handbook of Biblical Social Values*, 147–48.

39. Although the Mishnaic sources and Tosefta Megilla are from a later period, they reflect the oral tradition circulating among Second Temple Jews during the first century.

40. Herzog, *Jesus, Justice, and the Reign*, 119.

6. Disqualified priests (illegitimate children of priests)
7. *Netins* (temple slaves)
8. *Mamzers* (bastards)
9. Eunuchs
10. Those with damaged testicles; and
11. Those without a penis.[41]

Not unlike the map allocating pure space, the categories of personal holiness reach an apex with those who are closest to the temple.[42]

Galilean Perceptions

The financial circumstance of the majority class within the ancient world was desperate. Friesen's model concludes that more than 90 percent of the population within the Roman Empire existed near subsistent levels, and it can be argued this number was greater in Jewish Palestine.[43] C. C. McCown was one of the first scholars to adopt a strong, articulate position in terms of the impact of the agrarian society in first-century Palestine, determining that the population was "condemned" to "hard work and poverty" while utilizing the "crudest" methods of farming.[44] Furthermore, McCown assessed that, based on the unfortunate agricultural situation in combination with other economic disadvantages, it was a "miracle" that the subsistent population was able to survive.

The primary economic distinction among the Jewish providences was the presence of Jerusalem, the cultural hub, where the temple was located. Like its ancient counterparts, the temple in Jerusalem not only served the central function of religion and purification, but also as a financial institution.[45] The temple received the benefits of Herod's temple tax and elaborate gifts that would come from the far reaches of the East

---

41. Neyrey, "Idea of Purity Mark," 95–96.
42. This priority of the priest and Levite on the purity scale would have been automatically understood by early audiences of the good Samaritan, as well as the role of the Samaritan whose status was so low that he did not even merit an entry on the purity map.
43. Friesen, "Injustice or God's Will?," 19–20.
44. McCown, "Geography of Palestine," 626–29.
45. Oakman, *Political Aims of Jesus*, loc. 1776.

and West.⁴⁶ The temple's function as a focal point in society might have been made most visible through the construction efforts beginning with Herod the Great in 20 BCE, which ultimately lasted until 64 CE. As the purity map reflects, the wealth of Palestine and the broader Jewish world flowed toward Jerusalem and into the temple.

Jerusalem's geographic location was not an impressive agricultural area, nor part of any major trade route, and its distance from the coast further increased its economic disadvantages.⁴⁷ However, Goodman maintains that the noticeable prosperity of Jerusalem can be attributed to its religious role.⁴⁸ In large part, this was due to the annual pilgrimages wherein the city would enjoy the commercial prospects made available from widespread travelers.⁴⁹

While Jerusalem experienced economic benefits due to the various Herodian building projects, taxation, gifts, and pilgrimage festivals, an economic divide was created between this principal city and the surrounding regions of Judea and Galilee. This divide is well demonstrated by the contrast between the wealthy of each region. In Galilee, the ruling class lived much more modestly compared to their Judean counterparts.⁵⁰ This type of discrepancy tended to alienate the people of Galilee as it became difficult to distinguish the temple from the palace, as the priests and temple establishment were controlled by the king.⁵¹ Because of these socio-political dynamics, the temple failed to proportionally represent the overwhelmingly predominant peasant class, especially in Galilee, which resulted in discontented factions including anti-temple movements.⁵²

Interpreting the Parable according to Social Dynamics

This section presents three hermeneutical proposals and an interpretive hypothesis followed by the consideration of a key research question.

First, any interpretation of the Good Samaritan must consider the broader literary context, namely, Luke's travel narrative to Jerusalem that

---

46. Charlesworth, *Jesus and Temple*, 149.
47. Goodman, "Pilgrimage Economy of Jerusalem," 59.
48. Goodman, "Pilgrimage Economy of Jerusalem," 59.
49. Goodman, "Pilgrimage Economy of Jerusalem," 60.
50. Fiensy and Hawkins, *Galilean Economy*, 170.
51. Mathew, *Temple-Criticism Mark's Gospel*, 19.
52. Charlesworth, *Jesus and Temple*, 148.

CHAPTER 1: THE GOOD SAMARITAN IN SOCIAL-SCIENTIFIC PERSPECTIVE

takes place from Luke 9:51 to 19:27. These ten chapters form the literary core of Luke's Gospel. Throughout this portion, the author reiterates a persistent reminder that Jesus is on his way to Jerusalem. This demands for the interpreter to consider the Jerusalem context when interpreting the parable of the good Samaritan.

Second, Luke's presentation of financial ethics as taught by Jesus is largely unparalleled in the Gospel counterparts. Within the travel narrative is a very particular focus on economic dimensions. Much of the material in this section is exclusive to Luke and emphasizes ethics, including the parables of the good Samaritan (Luke 10:25–37), rich fool (Luke 12:13–21), prodigal son (Luke 15:11–32), rich man and Lazarus (Luke 16:19–31), in addition to the encounter with Zacchaeus (Luke 19:1–11).[53] Given this, the interpreter must also consider how relevant socio-economic considerations are to this parable.

The third hermeneutical key is that Jesus did engage in a temple protest (Luke 19:41–48) at the conclusion of this travel narrative. Therefore, this protest must be weighed as to its relevance when considering the role of the priest and Levite within the parable. An interpretive aid is found in Luke 19:46 in the clues Jesus gives when he references passages in Isa 56 and Jer 7. Each of the contexts treat ethics pertaining to greed and benevolence, suggesting that the temple is corrupted when ethics are ignored. Additionally, while there might be other symbolic elements to Jesus's actions, E. P. Sanders argues that Jesus turning over the tables while throwing out the money changers was a prophetic action designed to indicate the destruction that was to come.[54]

This chapter hypothesizes that the priest and Levite within the parable are intended to represent the temple establishment. Although this idea is less explored, it is not foreign to interpreters. Luke Timothy Johnson,[55] Joseph Fitzmyer,[56] and Diane Chen[57] contend that at least some representative characteristics are contained in the presentation of these characters within the parable. In addition, one cannot overstate Jesus's teachings regarding greed throughout the travel narrative as he "set his face" to the destination

---

53. Modern commentators have challenged the traditional, popularized titles for these parables, and rightfully so.
54. Sanders, *Jesus and Judaism*.
55. Johnson, *Gospel of Luke*, 173.
56. Fitzmyer, *Gospel according to Luke I–IX*, 884.
57. Chen, *Luke*, loc. 3924.

of Jerusalem (Luke 9:51), the location of the temple, which symbolized economic imbalance. Furthermore, Jesus's words and actions at the temple demonstrate a deep dissatisfaction with its economic function, suggesting the influence of anti-temple factions in Galilee.[58] Finally, during his protest, Jesus calls attention to contradiction of the temple establishment in Luke 19:46. Pilch's assessment that inconsistent group behavior led to impurity correlates with the idea that Jesus's protest is a way of articulating the impurity of the temple's ruling elite, and possibly the temple itself.[59]

To argue this hypothesis, it is imperative to ask whether Jesus used individuals as representatives of the larger population in prophetic or parabolic language. The answer is affirmed in several examples. Two instances, one prophetic and the other parabolic, are both contained within Luke's travel narrative. The first happening is an account that Jesus turns prophetic in Luke 13:1-5. Here, Jesus is asked about an occasion when Galileans suffered death in Jerusalem at the hands of Pilate. Jesus uses this report to deliver the stark prophetic announcement, "except you repent, you will likewise perish." N. T. Wright notes the following of this passage:

> The idea that Jesus was identifying with his fellow Jews as they faced imminent judgment is in fact inscribed into the larger narrative of Luke's Gospel as a whole. Particularly from chapter 9 on, Jesus is constantly warning his people of the great disaster that is hanging over their heads . . . "Unless you repent, you will all be destroyed in the same way" (13:1–5). In the same way. What does this mean? Jesus is not here speaking of people ending up in "hell" (Gehenna?) after their death . . . . He is speaking, rather, of Roman troops and falling buildings within Jerusalem, as he is again in the climactic warnings in 19:42–4, in his symbolic action in the Temple (19:45–46), and in his interpretation of that action in the following two chapters.[60]

The text clearly supports the idea that Jesus uses an isolated event and persons as a platform for as a symbolic pronouncement upon the broader whole.

---

58. As a note, there is strong evidence to support the idea that John the Baptist, an influencer of Jesus, taught an anti-temple message.

59. Pilch and Malina, *Handbook of Biblical Social Values*, 147–48. Interestingly enough, throughout the Lukan Gospel, Jesus's words and actions are declaring the unclean to have a newfound cleanliness; yet paradoxically, in the temple scene, it is as if he is declaring the status symbol of purity to be impure.

60. Wright, *Day the Revolution Began*, 215–16.

The second example is the story of the prodigal son (Luke 15:11–32), in which Jesus uses the narrative to represent a broader point. Wright argues that the prodigal son illustrates the story of wider Israel returning from physical exile. Furthermore, the call for a vast amount spiritual exiles in Jesus's day to return home was represented by each account of individual healing and forgiveness in the Gospels.[61]

Following the same line of study illustrated in these brief examples, it is hermeneutically justifiable to argue that Jesus used individuals as representatives of a broader class of people in his pronouncements. This establishes literary precedent for the hypothesis concerning the priest and Levite as representatives of the failed temple establishment in the parable of the good Samaritan.

Conclusion

Within the parable of the good Samaritan, the priest and Levite represent the temple establishment and how disconnected they are from the traveler. In addition, following the sequence of the purity map, Jesus's audience might have expected a ruling Jew or even commoner to follow the priest and Levite. Instead, Jesus's rhetoric is to present an extreme that is off the scale of the purity chart by invoking the presence of the unclean Samaritan. This continues the reversal theme found in the same Gospel. Meanwhile, by upholding the Samaritan as the positive example in the stead of the temple elite, Jesus instructs the inquisitive lawyer as to what kind of person a neighbor truly is in a world with kinship at the core of the people's socially conscious minds.[62]

---

61. Wright, *Jesus and the Victory of God*, 177–82.
62. Gordon Fee believes Jesus engaged with a Pharisee in this parable. If so, the conclusion that the good neighbor was a Samaritan would have been even more of a stark lesson given how the Pharisaic party existed to maintain Jewish purity. See Fee and Stuart, *How to Read the Bible*, 155.

Chapter 2: A Social-Scientific Reading of Zechariah's Status Reversal in Luke 1:5–25

IN HIS TWO-VOLUME WORK, Luke has compiled what amounts to the largest contribution to the New Testament corpus, accounting for roughly 27 percent of the material.[1] Luke was a sophisticated presenter, a literary artist who carefully designed and structured his writings. Unsurprisingly, as with any such material, the introduction to the Lukan Gospel, the lengthiest among New Testament books, presents clues to the essential truths that will be conveyed in Luke's two volumes.

Furthermore, Luke's introductory matter represents a valuable source with its unique inclusion of the angelic announcements to both Zechariah (1:5–25) and Mary (1:26–38); speeches from Mary (1:46–56), Elizabeth (1:41–45), and Zechariah (1:67–79); the birth narrative (2:1–21); and the double temple scene (2:22–51).

As with Acts, the bookends of the Gospel concentrate on Jerusalem and the temple, indicative of the importance of these topics to Luke and generating rich theological dialogue.[2] This chapter concentrates on the

---

1. This chapter was first presented as a paper read at the Eastern Regional Meeting of the Evangelical Theological Society at Regent University School of Divinity on April 23, 2022.

2. In Luke, 1:5–26 takes place at the Jerusalem temple, then in 1:39–56 Mary travels near to Jerusalem and remains there three months, then the birth of John the Baptist (1:5–80) is near Jerusalem. Moreover, Jesus's birth (2:1–21) occurs near Jerusalem, and the remainder of Luke 2 (2:22–51) happens at Jerusalem. The conclusion of Luke (19:28–53) is in or near Jerusalem. Additionally, Acts opens in Jerusalem (1:1—8:2) and before extending outwardly and then near the conclusion, there is a high quantity of material with Paul's travel and arrest in the same city (20:1—26:32).

CHAPTER 2: ZECHARIAH'S STATUS REVERSAL IN LUKE 1:5–25

front matter of the Lukan corpus, which begins with Zechariah, a priest, in Jerusalem, receiving the announcement regarding the forthcoming birth of John the Baptist. Meanwhile, the Gospel concludes following temple scenes in Jerusalem where Jesus is martyred not unlike the baptizer. This study surveys Luke's overall tone regarding the priesthood throughout Luke-Acts before demonstrating Luke's intentionality in crafting the narrative of Zechariah to foreshadow status reversal regarding the temple and the priesthood.

The Priesthood in Luke-Acts

Before making exegetical observations of social contexts of Luke's first chapter, it is helpful to initially summarize Luke's view of priests in his two-volume work. The most positive attribution comes in Acts 6:7 where several anonymous priests respond favorably to the apostles' preaching. However, the author articulates in repetition in Acts the continued resistance of the apostolic movement by the chief priests and high priest of Jerusalem. This is demonstrated in the early detainment and arrest of Peter and John in Acts 3–5. Furthermore, the seizure of Stephen in Acts 6–7 is also enacted under the auspices of the priest. Moreover, Saul of Tarsus is said to have been granted the permission of the high priest to arrest early members of the church (9:1–2), an account that Saul continues to echo in his later testimonies (22:5; 26:10–12). Finally, in Acts, Saul himself becomes a victim of attempted murder by the priests late in the narrative (23:2, 14–15; 25:2–3).[3]

In his Gospel, Luke distinctly articulates Jesus's anticipation of rejection in Jerusalem by the chief priests (9:22), which is then realized at the conclusion of his travel narrative when the elite priests resist Jesus, place him on trial, and become largely responsible for his death (19:4; 20:1, 19; 22:2, 4, 52–54, 66; 23:1–5, 23; 24:20).[4] The rest of the material concerning priests is sparse, but hardly presents any positivity concerning the sect. In Luke 10:30–35, the parable of the good Samaritan offers a view of a priest who neglects his ultimate duty. In Luke 5:14 and 17:14, Jesus instructs the beneficiaries of healing to show themselves to the priests, an endeavor

---

3. Furthermore, an additional negative presentation of the priests occurs with the seven sons of Sceva, the high priest, in Acts 19:13–16 who are shamed after being impotent with handling an unclean spirit.

4. Jesus's parable of the tenants in Luke 20:9–19 was directed toward the priests for their failures and abuses of power.

necessary for them to be reinstituted within regular social categories. These two occasions merely acknowledge the priests' function in society, rather than indicating Luke's view of them. Still, it is appropriate to note that the exemplar model of the Samaritan leper in Luke 17:11–19, who returns to give thanks unlike his nine Jewish counterparts, would not have been able to receive a clean bill of health from the priesthood due to the Samaritan alienation from the Jerusalem temple cult. Perhaps Luke intends a greater theological indication with the inclusion of this estranged character, as this is the second time when the virtue of a non-temple-participating Samaritan is extolled in contrast to the limitations of a priest.

An additional mention of the priesthood occurs in Luke 3:2 when Luke references Annas and Caiaphas, who are named primarily as time markers, but this association prompts a reminder of these widely considered unpopular characters. The only other mention of a priest is the case of Zechariah, which offers nuances that shall be further entertained.

Even given the positive mention of the priests converting to faith in Acts, Luke-Acts' overall presentation paints a negative picture of the priesthood, primarily expressed through the priests' actions toward Jesus and the later disciple groups. Furthermore, the failure of the priest in the good Samaritan, the inability of the assumed priest in Luke 17:11–19 to reintegrate a leper into society, and the punishment of Zechariah in Luke 1:5–25, which will be subsequently explained, all add a tremendously negative weight to the author's depiction of this profession.

Socio-Historical Insight—The Priesthood

The reason for Luke's critical presentation is likely both theological and literary. He presents the early Christian movement as being directed away from Jerusalem, in contrast to the historical Hebrew practice, which was focused on the city with religious pilgrimages and tithes being funneled toward the temple. Furthermore, if Luke was a gentile, or even a Hellenistic Jew, these factors would shed further light on why the temple cult would not serve his primary interests.

In addition, Luke's view of the priesthood may have been reinforced, if not influenced, by many long-standing social contexts in the first century, as reflected by Second Temple period Jewish texts. From the time of King David, high priests had been selected from the lineage of Zadok; however, this practice ends in 174 BCE when Antiochus Epiphanes is bribed to replace the high priest.[5] Furthermore, the Maccabean revolt in 171 paved the way for the Hasmonean line of priests. From this period forward, texts reiterate the corruption and bribery associated with the high priestly office.

Later, the Romans would continue to reinforce the temple-state set up by the Persian occupation, enabling the priesthood to serve in critical political and economic functions. Rome, or a client king from the Herodian dynasty, would select the Jewish high priest since the office fell under Roman patronage. Furthermore, during the time of Herod the Great, priests were known to make sacrifices on behalf of Herod toward Rome and Caesar. Given the political association of the high priestly position, it is unsurprising that twenty-seven individuals filled the position in the 105 years between 37 BCE and 68 CE, around the time of Luke's writing.[6] Only three served more than five years. The longest tenured was Joseph Caiaphas, who filled the role for seventeen years, nearly twice as long as anyone else likely due to his compliance with the Roman and Herodian powers. Incidentally, the politically aligned Caiaphas was the high priest during the trial of Jesus.

The Herodian Dynasty under Roman supervision was the temple's primary patron, organizing a construction project that lasted decades whereby the temple's architecture took on a Hellenistic design, and Roman insignia had previously been placed on its premises, while the Antonia Fortress, which at times housed the Roman army, was in immediate proximity. This not only served to defile the grounds in the minds of many, but also tainted the compliant priests.

The vast peasant majority was burdened with supporting three areas of governance: Rome, Herod, and the priestly aristocracy, the latter supported by the half shekel temple tax required of all men as well as additional tithes. The priesthood policed Jerusalem with a temple guard, not only to protect themselves, but also to enforce the seizure of tithes, with recorded examples of these aggressive actions from antiquity.[7] Further evidence suggests that the upper-class priests became wealthy land patrons, a status which produced additional income in terms of rent from sharecroppers and portions of the produced crop, even while there was no provision in the Hebrew scriptures allocating land ownership to the Levitical tribe.[8] This detail does not escape Luke as he reflects Barnabas in Acts, a Levite, as possessing land,

---

5. Hays, *Temple and Tabernacle*, 162–63.
6. VanderKam, *Joshua to Caiaphas*, loc. 8174.
7. Horsley, *Jesus and Empire*, loc. 590–92.
8. Montero, *All Things in Common*, 8.

which is later liquidated with the proceeds benefiting the *ecclesia* (Acts 4:36–37). Because of their position, the priesthood, most specifically the elitists in Jerusalem, came to represent what was wrong in society—Roman occupation, Herodian rule, an exploitative economy, and a temple that failed to socio-economically represent the majority class.

These dynamics prompted numerous resistance movements, not merely against Rome but also the temple and its hierarchy. At the extremes history locates communities like the Essenes at Qumran who saw their collective as a substitute not only for the temple, but for Jewish society altogether. In addition, N. T. Wright claims that even the Pharisees developed their rituals and devotion to Torah as a temple alternative.[9] Of course, John the Baptizer, who will be addressed more specifically later in this chapter, offered a movement regarding the forgiveness of sins comparable to but apart from that of the temple. Meanwhile, more violent reactions included the Fourth Philosophy, and later zealots, who rose to prominence during Luke's lifetime, taking decisive and direct action against the temple and its priests.

These are not mere historical factors; these elements engendered a longstanding lack of trust between the widespread populace toward the priesthood. Examples of this distrust are reflected in literature. In 1 Enoch (89:73, 94–105) the priesthood is observed as oppressing the poor and defiling sacrifices, and this text assesses that it is necessary for a new temple to emerge. First and Second Maccabees (1 Macc 4:14, 14:41, 2 Macc 2:7) describe a polluted temple needing to be restored. The Psalms of Solomon (2:1–3, 11–12; 8:10–12) assert that the temple was not only polluted by the priest's dishonest business dealings, but the priests themselves were also defiled through unlawful sexual behavior including joining themselves to prostitutes. The commentary on Habakkuk (2:5–6) found at Qumran references a Wicked Priest corrupted by wealth and power who engages in impure practices and harms the populace. The Apocalypse of Weeks (89:73) remarks on the eternal temple to arrive that will replace the one of defiled sacrifices. Jubilees (1:15–17) affirms that YHWH's return will coincide with a new temple. The Temple Scroll (29:8) and Sibylline Oracles (3:294, 3:702–20) speak of a forthcoming eschatological temple. Finally, even the later Talmud traditions (b. Pesah. 57a) rebuke priests for oppressive activity.

The abuse of power by the priesthood, reflected in some Second Temple–era texts, contains not only specific moral infractions via sexual

---

9. Wright, *Jesus and the Victory of God*, 522.

deviancy, but other ethical infringements, primarily concerning wealth and material possessions, a theme that is of tremendous import to Luke.

Socio-Historical Insight—The New Temple

While all the various nuances can hardly be explored in this chapter; Luke-Acts maintains quite an interest in a new temple paradigm. The broad direction of the book of Acts presents the flow of the early church's movement in contrasting terms with the purity map of their time. Note the Mishnah, Kelim 1:6–933:

> The land of Israel is holier than any other land.
>
> The walled cities [of the land of Israel] are holier still . . .
>
> Within the walls of Jerusalem is still more holy . . .
>
> The Temple Mount is still more holy . . .
>
> The Rampart [surrounding the Temple precincts] is still more holy . . .
>
> The Court of the Women is still more holy . . .
>
> The Court of the Israelites is still more holy . . .
>
> The Court of the Priests is still more holy . . .
>
> Between the Porch and the Altar is still more holy . . .
>
> The sanctuary [the holy place] is still more holy . . .
>
> And the Holy of Holies is still more holy . . . .[10]

Namely, as an alternate temple group, the *ecclesia* was not focused on pilgrimaging toward Jerusalem, according to temple requirements, but rather on branching outward, "to the ends of the earth" (Acts 1:8) in conscious juxtaposition to the Judaism that birthed the Jesus movement. Moreover, throughout Acts, the temple progressively loses emphasis, except in cases in which unjust trials occur. The lengthiest speech in Acts is that of Stephen (7:2–53), who among other things affirms the God of mobility, representative of tabernacle behavior, while warning that the Jerusalem temple has become an idol.

---

10. Herzog, *Jesus, Justice, and the Reign*, 119.

Socio-Historical Insight—The Physical Orifice

Returning to the introduction of Luke, the textual evidence initially presents Zechariah and Elizabeth in terms of a high moral pedigree, attributing to them the righteousness of being good commandment keepers (1:6). Zechariah is of the lineage of Aaron as prescribed in Exodus, suggesting him to be a legitimate priest (1:5). Adding further to the qualifications of this household is that Elizabeth is also from the line of Aaron (1:5). The marriage of a priest to a fellow daughter of Aaron was not a necessity but likely desirable. With these descriptors, this couple's religious status is affirmed, as well as their ascribed honor, the result of genealogy.

An additional source of honor would have been derived from the couple's advanced age (1:7). Not only did senior years afford a good standing in their culture's honor paradigm, but it was also less common in a world where life spans were remarkably limited. In the case of the latter, the brevity of life was typically compounded by complication of childbirth by under-matured and malnourished bodies; however, this was an obstacle from which the childless Elizabeth was exempt (1:7).

This fact draws the focus from the honorable dimension of the couple toward the contrasting shameful portion of the narrative. Without a doubt, in the modern Western world, being without children should not be a social or theological barometer of shame; however, the necessity of childbearing was a socio-economic bedrock of the world of the text.

Space does not permit fully expounding upon this, but the world of antiquity did not face the obstacle of overpopulation; rather, it viewed everything as being in limited supply, even people.[11] This was the natural result of the various factors leading to a diminished life span. One means by which individuals contributed toward the stabilization of the social group was through bearing offspring. Furthermore, children were the primary form of social security in a world without benefits for the retired. Additionally, widows without sons were often exploited since their husband's wealth and possessions, most often in the form of land, required transference to a male relative, thus creating urgency to have as many children as possible to secure a direct descendant as a future male head of household. There is biblical precedent for establishing such a social imperative. Luke 1–2 makes several allusions to Hannah from 1 Sam 1, who is desperate for children

---

11. Neyrey, "Limited Good," 103–6.

CHAPTER 2: ZECHARIAH'S STATUS REVERSAL IN LUKE 1:5–25

even when her husband begs the foolish question, "Am I not better than 10 sons?" (1 Sam 1:8) with the understood answer to be a resounding no!

Other social dynamics come into play regarding the concept of barrenness. Mary Douglas rightly assesses the correlation between the physical and social orifices.[12] The Hebrew scripture maintains quite an interest in purity concerns regarding the physical orifices—specifically, what enters and exits the body through the mouth, including food eaten following the washing of hands, and what is expelled by the body even in terms of menstruation, ejaculation, and birthing fluids. Skin diseases identified in the Gospels, such as leprosy, were considered severe impairments to purity because they created unnatural entry and escape points, or body openings.

Mary Douglas explains that societies with a strong emphasis on regulating the physical orifices would enlist the physical body in this way as a surrogate for the social body.[13] Cultural sub-groups that saw themselves as threatened and vulnerable in a larger society restricted the entry to and exit from their social body, limiting influences on the body politic. Simply put, whether it was historical impositions from Egypt, Babylon, Canaanite culture and religion, or, in the first-century perspective, the allowances of Hellenism, Rome, or errant Jews, many sects were concerned with whom and what they permitted to enter their social orifices. Accordingly, those concerns ruled portions of society and controlled those who were required to exit the social body due to being considered unclean in the physical body. This, in part, begins to explain, though not justify, some of the strict regulations and potentially inhumane treatment by Jesus's opponents of disabled persons depicted in the biblical texts. Furthermore, in some Second Temple texts, priests were accused of engaging in sexual intercourse with menstruating partners.[14] While it is uncertain as to how this evidence was apprehended, however, it speaks to the overlap of ritual and moral purity that surrounded concerns over the orifices.

Returning to consider Zechariah and Elizabeth, barrenness, to some degree, was seen as a flaw of the physical orifice. Are sexual relations physically nothing more than the invasion of one orifice by another whereby the success of the process is determined by the escape from the male orifice and its ability to merge with the product of the female orifice? Therefore, if success in conception is dependent on proper function of bodily orifices,

---

12. Douglas, *Purity and Danger*, 144.
13. Douglas, *Purity and Danger*, 144.
14. See Psalms of Solomon 2:1–3, 11–12; 8:10–12.

then when the process fails, are the orifices not to blame? The answer is yes; and in the ancient world, the womb of the woman was viewed as the culprit. This deduction is the first detractor from the positive honor status of Zechariah and Elizabeth. It is far more than a subtle takeaway; it is a glowing reminder of the limitations of their success, as without a son it was expected that Zechariah's noble genealogy would cease with him.

The second detractor is found Zechariah's words in 1:18, in his direct response to Gabriel's announcement. There is scriptural precedent of announced births in the case of Isaac, also born to aging parents; of Samson (Judg 13:1–25), whose Nazarite vows echo that of the description to Zechariah; and of Samuel (1 Sam 1:1–28), whose more nuanced blessing occurs by the priest at the tent of the Lord, the antecedent of the temple. However, it seems that Zechariah has missed this connection, and his response to the angel is portrayed as less innocent than Mary's later words.

Gabriel assesses in his response that Zechariah lacks belief (1:20). The usage of *pisteuo* occurs sparsely in Luke-Acts and is often employed in such a way where an individual is directly confronted concerning their lack of belief. In a theological sense, this portrayal begins to blemish Zechariah's status of righteousness. What follows tarnishes his social status tremendously; he is silenced, *siopao* (1:20), not only in his mouth but, Luke 1:62 suggests, in his ears as well, given that they must communicate to him through writings.

This is a punitive action, and within the honor-shame dimensions of antiquity, having one's voice and mouth overpowered is quite shameful. In such a world, public speech is the role of men, and eloquence is a male virtue; in contrast, Zechariah now becomes passive and dishonored. Meanwhile the text conveys that his wife must speak for him. Furthermore, recalling how the care of the physical orifices are strongly associated with purity and cleanliness in Hebrew thinking, it is evident that what has occurred to Zechariah is a defilement. His orifices are now polluted because they do not function properly.

This character has started off with the appearance of being righteous and favorable, but his honor level becomes quite poor as the evidence is compiled. The large crowd that Luke describes as waiting for Zechariah to exit the temple grows concerned (1:21), and as he does depart, he does so unable to hear or speak. As he emerges from the temple, he is unable to offer any words or priestly blessing. It may appear to some that judgment has fallen upon him for entering the temple unworthily, in what was possibly the first and only time of his life having served immediately at the altar. Publicly, this may even have been seen as substantiating the childlessness of this priest. This is a very dishonorable and polluted treatment of this character.

Leviticus 21:16–23 restricts the functions of blemished or physically defective priests, a category into which Zechariah now falls. Moreover, this is especially alarming since physical defects were associated with defective sacrifices and blemished morality within that Levitical text. As previously outlined, literature produced in the Second Temple period indicates that priests were already highly suspect, and now Zechariah appears even more so.

Further scriptural nuances are connected to the ears and mouth. Exodus 29:20, Lev 8:23–24 and 14:14, 17, 25, 28 describe a liturgical component of a priestly rite performed by placing blood on the ear lobes. In these instances, the ear is associated with the purification and consecration of the priest. Ears also become a critical consideration in Stephen's speech from Acts 7 (51, 57) when, placed on trial by the high priest, in giving a message about the idolatry of the temple cult, he observes their uncircumcised ears. Sometimes ears are nothing more than ears, but this orifice is theologically significant to Luke.

The mouth also tends to be highly theological as that orifice is a primary extension of personhood. Perhaps most remarkable is that while Zechariah's mouth and access to full priesthood functions are closed, Elizabeth's womb, and as equally important, her mouth, are simultaneously opened. Socially and even theologically speaking, Zechariah is shamed while Elizabeth confesses her shame to be removed (1:25).

Are there some hints to circumcision here? Likely not; however, in Acts, Stephen's remarks regarding uncircumcision relate this marker associated with the male sexual organ to the ears as well. The ears are primarily a receptor, not unlike the womb. Meanwhile, Zechariah's receptor has been closed, while Elizabeth's receptor, her womb, a part of her sexual personification not unlike the male foreskin, has been blessed and opened. This is an exploratory feature at best. What is more concrete is that the case of Zechariah and Elizabeth reflects a clear status reversal, a hallmark theme in Luke-Acts.

Status Reversal in Jewish Society

The conceptuality of purity in ancient Judaism remarkably categorizes both persons and locations according to degrees of holiness. Unsurprisingly, all statuses of men are elevated above women. Of the men, Levites are the purest, and among the Levites, the holiest segment of ancient Judaism were priests like Zechariah. This status was ascribed in conjunction with their services in the holiest of cities, Jerusalem, at the most sacred location, the temple, and the priests' access to navigate the most holy places of that temple. The Tosefta Megilla reflects perceptions of first-century Judaism with its organization of persons noted below:

1. Priests
2. Levites
3. Israelites
4. Converts (proselytes)
5. Freed slaves
6. Disqualified priests (illegitimate children of priests)
7. *Netins* (temple slaves)
8. *Mamzers* (bastards)
9. Eunuchs
10. Those with damaged testicles; and
11. Those without a penis.[15]

Accordingly, Zechariah was symbolic of the most sacred persons and the most holy location on the ancient map, yet he becomes shamed. However, Elizabeth, being a woman, and a barren woman at that, now finds her status reversed in juxtaposition with her husband. Strikingly, the first human voice in the Lukan corpus to introduce the gospel message and give testimony is this previously shamed woman (1:25). Noteworthy as this may be, it is even more so when contrasted with the voice of the male priest Zechariah, the first human voice to speak at all in the narrative, which gives a doubtful response rather than theological affirmation, and is silenced.

---

15. Neyrey, "Idea of Purity Mark," 95–96.

CHAPTER 2: ZECHARIAH'S STATUS REVERSAL IN LUKE 1:5-25

Status Reversal—Elizabeth

Elizabeth exemplifies the right response to what is occurring within the Lukan narrative, while Zechariah initially serves as the antithesis. Elizabeth's voice is an indicator of status reversal, so common to Luke where the humble are exalted and the great humbled (14:11, 18:14), and where the last become first at the expense of the first who are reversed (13:30). Statuses of the wealthy are reversed with the poor (6:20), the hungry with the fed (6:21), men with women in addition to other marginalized characters. Not only does the high-status priestly Zechariah present qualities that the author desires to illustrate in contrast in the Lukan reversal motif, but his newfound shameful status also highlights that the Holy Spirit and the angelic announcement point to this child as not the product of the mere success of Zechariah and Elizabeth, but of the hand of God. There are also indications that Elizabeth is the first in Luke-Acts to be filled with the Holy Spirit, in a method typical of the Lukan writings in which the Spirit and speech are inevitably connected.[16]

Status Reversal—Mary

The motif combining this great reversal with gospel proclamation continues in this introductory chapter with Mary, who is the second born person to receive the Holy Spirit filling.[17] While the priest, representing the purity core of society, is silenced, Luke makes a point to articulate when women or daughters prophesy (Acts 2:17). Mary's young voice from what appears to be a modest background becomes the most active and expressive in the early Gospel through her Magnificat (1:46–55), which is ignited by Elizabeth's remarks to her (1:39–45). Again, eloquence of speech was a male virtue; while Zechariah is silenced, Mary's eloquence is highlighted in that section.

---

16. The reasoning is that if John the Baptized is filled with the Holy Spirit from Elizabeth's womb, as indicated by Gabriel (1:15), then pragmatically, his mother would also have been filled. Moreover, Elizabeth is the initial person in the Lukan corpus directly stated to be filled with the Spirit (1:41).

17. Luke makes a clear point of presenting Jesus as superior to John the Baptist. Given this, one must presume that since Elizabeth is filled with the Spirit, then Mary must also be. Moreover, since Spirit filling and speech are so heavily tied together in Luke-Acts, Mary's Magnificat (1:46–55) is evidence of the prophetic Spirit upon her.

In this narrative, Mary becomes a traveler, in what could be speculated as a liberating move for a young woman, making her way from the northern areas of Galilee toward the region of Jerusalem where Elizabeth resided (1:39–45). Again, in Luke-Acts, journeying is something akin to a theological virtue, because Luke portrays the early church as mobile tabernacle in contrast with the stationary temple. This is reflected in various ways, from Jesus's travel narrative to Jerusalem beginning in Luke 9:51, to Jesus's declaration of the mission to the ends of the earth in Acts 1:8, to the new diaspora in Acts 8:2 following Stephen's stoning, which prompts the dispersion of the gospel, and eventually to Paul's missionary travels, which conclude with a travel motif back to Jerusalem and then to Rome.

The deeper implications of Mary's role in this great reversal are even more remarkable. In this narrative, the priestly male, Zechariah, remains dysfunctional. However, the women theologically appear to be at the inner core of the holy sanctum, a place reserved for priests. Some work has been conducted regarding the parallels between this portion of Luke 1:39–45 and the return of the Ark of the Covenant in 2 Sam 6. John McHugh elucidates:

> The two stories open with the statement that David and Mary "arose and made a journey" up into the hill country, into the land of Judah. On arrival, both the Ark and Mary are greeted with "shouts" of joy. In the Septuagint, the verb used for Elizabeth's greeting in Luke 1:42 is used only in connection with liturgical ceremonies centered round the Ark. The Ark, on its way to Jerusalem, was taken into the house of Obed-edom and became a source of blessing for his house; Mary's entry into the house of Elizabeth is also seen as a source of blessing for the house. David, in terror at the untouchable holiness of the Ark, cried out: "How shall the Ark of the Lord come to me?"; Elizabeth, in awe before the mother of her Lord, says, "Why should this happen to me, that the mother of my Lord should come to me?" Finally, we read that "the Ark of the Lord remained in the house of Obed-edom three months," and that Mary stayed with Elizabeth "about three months."[18]

If one takes this compelling parallel as theologically conclusive, then one must infer that Mary is at least a steward of the ark of God, in a similar fashion to a priest. A more robust view is that perhaps Mary becomes an ark herself, even holier than the priest, and in accordance with the already mentioned purity categories, she represents the most sacred person, object, and location among creation. With either deduction, here the motif of

---

18. McHugh, *Mother of Jesus*, 62.

reversal in Luke's first chapter is compounded. The priest is dysfunctional with physical impairments, not suitable for the social body, and the substitutions in speech and priestly service are the unlikely women.

Status Reversal—John the Baptizer

Elizabeth herself is stewarding a priest inside of her, one who seemingly will fail to follow in the traditional footsteps of his father. Why is this? Luke does tend to highlight sons who venture independently, including the prodigal son (Luke 15:11–32); Peter and the sons of Zebedee, who seemingly abandon their inherited trades; and Jesus at Nazareth, who was rejected in Nazareth in part because his words to them alienated himself (Luke 4:22–29). In Luke 9:59–62 when he begins his journey to Jerusalem, there are those who want to bury fathers or at least say goodbye to family, whom Jesus seems to become abrasive with. Even in Luke 11:27–28, when a voice from the crowd responding positively to his teachings proclaims "a blessing on the womb that bore you and the breasts you nursed," Jesus counters with blessings on those who hear and do God's words.

Perhaps through John the Baptizer, it continues to signify the reversal in terms of the quality of priesthood. John seems to be instituting a new priesthood, out in the wilderness as with the household of Aaron in the exodus account, bringing people back through the Jordan River and calling them to widespread purity in that ceremonial cleansing (Luke 3:2–20). Most remarkable is that the forgiveness of sins, something that was formerly legitimated through the actions of the temple cult, is now made openly available. John's social independence from his household amounted to a rejection of his genealogy, thus adding a further shameful element to Zechariah; however, theologically, John represents the fulfillment of the line of Aaron.

While Zechariah is shamed and his vocation temporarily placed in jeopardy, on a positive note, he benefits at the conclusion when his newly found shame is reversed, and he becomes an oracle of God. Each of these components seems to be at the short-term expense of Zechariah in what amounts to a compelling drama.

Conclusion

In the unique material that introduces his two volumes, Luke emphasizes the theological agendas of a replacement temple and priesthood through narrative instances of status reversal, with special attention given to the role of females in contrast with Zechariah as representative of the temple and the priesthood. Zechariah is Luke's first demonstration of this role reversal, foreshadowing events that will soon happen in the kingdom of God. Eventually Zechariah is filled with the Holy Spirit (1:67) and does speak, supplying his Benedictus (1:67–79), but only after the doubly reinforced female voice is heard.[19] Furthermore, the priest, at the societal core, only receives the Holy Spirit filling following the aged and formerly barren Elizabeth, the young virgin Mary, and the infant child John the Baptist. The author's point is not to permanently denigrate Zechariah, but to present him as symbol of reversal to type him as a character alluding to the questionable role of priests and religious leaders in the remainder of the two-volume work. The one who was positioned as the holiest in society becomes last, indicating a strategic reordering of many religious perspectives within the new temple paradigm.

---

19. In Luke 1:40, it is as if Zechariah is omitted from the story when Mary enters the home, and Luke only describes that Elizabeth is greeted and engaged. Moreover, in 1:57–66, Luke expresses Zechariah's public shamed as he describes the people celebrating and rejoicing with Elizabeth while her husband's name is omitted. Moreover, the crowds are content to converse with her initially regarding the naming of John, something distinctly out of protocol in Jewish life, yet they only "make signs" to Zechariah, soliciting his input when the expectations of the community are disrupted by the seemingly strange name Elizabeth proposes.

Chapter 3: The Progression of Controversy and Response in Mark 1:21—3:6 with Implications for Lukan Redaction

In a 1973 *Journal of Biblical Literature* article entitled "The Literacy Structure of the Controversy Stories in Mark 2:1—3:6," Joanna Dewey articulates a strong literary connection among the conflict stories early in Mark's Gospel.[1] She recognizes this structure as beginning with Jesus's healing of a man with paralysis in Mark 2:1 and lasting through the Sabbath conflicts ending in Mark 3:6.[2] Dewey develops chiastic correlations and literary qualities within these pericopes to enhance her argument that these narratives are intended to form a unit.

This chapter furthers Dewey's findings by expanding the unit to include Mark 1:40–45, while contributing to narrative features of each pericope conveying escalated controversy scenes in the personality of Jesus's words and actions and the critical responses of his audiences. The concluding section considers Luke's maintenance of this Markan order of these events, even while Matthew elected to disrupt them, as the narrative components substantiate Luke's theological priorities.

---

1. Dewey, "Controversy Stories Mark 2:1–3:6," 394–401.

2. This presentation was initially delivered on March 11, 2022, at the at the Mid-Atlantic Regional (virtual) Meeting of the Society for Biblical Literature.

Pericope 1: Healing the Leper (Mark 1:40–45)

Scenario

The initial pericope investigated is Mark 1:40–45, when Jesus heals a man with leprosy, a compelling basis for the increasing tension in the next three scenarios.

Social Implications

Skin disease is a prime example of the social and religious purity ritualistic concerns that Jesus faced. The nuances of societal response to those diseased were debated in antiquity, and it is an active conversation among contemporary scholarship with competing theories regarding how first-century Judaism regarded impurities and skin disease. One view is that purity restrictions for these diseases were widespread, resulting in absolute isolation of the sick. However, within the Old Testament, ritual purity correlates primarily with temple conduct and preparation and to a lesser degree with routine life. Additionally, Myrick Shinall argues that the degrees of social exclusion of those with skin disorders varied within different communities.[3] While Shinall's findings are nuanced, and perhaps overstated, due diligence requires an acknowledgment of competing theories. Also, while noting that the Torah declares skin impairments as unclean, it does not identify anyone as sinful for having touched a person with such a condition.

These three perspectives—the greater emphasis on purity relating to temple conduct rather than everyday life; the varying practices of imposed purity restrictions in different communities; and the distinction between ritual and moral impurities—are necessary to balance the improprieties of past and present commentators who have made aggressive assertions and assumptions regarding Jewish law and practice. Perhaps the most balanced and appropriate view is to recognize that modern divisions on these issues are a result of the variety of ancient viewpoints.

Joel Marcus rightly notes some evidence in Mark 1:40–45 of at least subtle controversy connected with the healing in this passage. More precisely, the hint of discordance within this narrative comes from touching the man with a skin disease. What is certain is that the Hebrew text is

---

3. Shinall, "Social Condition of Lepers," 915–34.

CHAPTER 3: CONTROVERSY AND RESPONSE IN MARK 1:21—3:6

concerned with boundaries and protocol for those with skin impairments, notably in Lev 13–14 and Num 12:9–15. As Marcus observes, these legal standards and their later interpretations mirror instructions for "the same sort of defilement as touching dead bodies," making this affliction a serious social concern.[4]

The uncomfortable impropriety of handling skin disease on a social level supports the identification of this healing as a precursor leading into the more direct and obviously controversial stories that occur subsequently within this unit.[5] In her critical works on Levitical purity concerns from a socio-anthropological perspective, Mary Douglas maintains that for many ancient cultures, including the Hebrews, the physical orifices become a surrogate for the body politic.[6] In essence, the great degree of concern regarding the opening of the social body, over who or what may enter or exit the collective, is likewise translated to a strict observation of rules regarding the openings of the physical body. From a socio-historical point of view, the Jewish social "orifices" in first-century Palestine were under extreme threat. The source was many-faceted, including a series of imperial impositions resulting in exile and return, the introduction of Hellenism, and eventually the myriad of socio-political concerns erupting from the Roman occupation, including Herodian politics.

These threats to Jewish identity generated a considerable amount of resistance that manifested via the formation of various sub-societies. These included the Qumran sect, which professed the purpose of living out true purity; the Pharisees, who maintained a guard over the physical and social orifices; and the Fourth Philosophy and later zealots, who formed combative groups responding to hostile socio-political circumstances. Because of this complexity, as this study will reiterate, it is wise not to overgeneralize qualities as pertaining to all of first-century Judaism. However, the social situation meant that some Jewish groups in that setting certainly placed an emphasis on ritual purity as a means to preserve the collective from cultural invaders, foreign and domestic.

While Jesus's healing this skin disease plants him somewhere within the debate over purity issues, the only definitive indication of the Markan text is that Jesus cures the disease, which should greatly reduce the social concern since the skin disease is no longer present following the event.

---

4. Marcus, *Mark 1–8*, 208.
5. Marcus, *Mark 1–8*, 207.
6. Douglas, *Purity and Danger*, 144.

Therefore, this obstacle is present but will prove to be the least serious of the controversial issues in this series of stories. Moreover, this story presents the opportunity to demonstrate the man's faith in Jesus, as the leper asks for help, saying to Jesus, "If you are willing, you can make me clean" (1:40).

Opposition and Response

The opposition to Jesus and his reaction are muted in this initial story in the series. Jesus's opponents take no action; however, the threat of their antagonism is present. Hints of controversy emerge when Jesus instructs the cured man to approach the priest to secure his social reintegration with an offering as instructed by the Torah yet gives him a directive to remain silent about Jesus's involvement (1:42–43). Then, when word spreads regardless of this warning, Jesus is "no longer able to enter any town openly but stayed outside in remote places" (1:45). Although people keep coming to him as he retreats into temporary semi-isolation, Jesus's warning and subsequent reaction infer an awareness of inherent danger from his opposition without stating it outright.

Pericope 2: Forgiving Sins (Mark 2:1–11)

Scenario

In Mark 2:1–11, the second pericope, the narrative provides a stark and immediate contrast to the prior story. First, the setting is specific; Jesus is in Capernaum in a home. Second, as word has spread, so has the audience, so he is under increased scrutiny in a more public situation. The social and religious context, the objections, and Jesus's actions present greater stakes. In the prior story regarding the leper, skin disease relates to ritual impurity, but not to sin. In contrast, although Jesus heals a paralytic in this story, the primary dilemma surrounds the forgiveness of sins, since the affliction of paralysis was at times associated with sin according to the view of the ancient world.

Social Implications

Assessing the cultural view in the ancient world of those who suffered with a disability is a complex and sensitive topic. At least in some cases,

CHAPTER 3: CONTROVERSY AND RESPONSE IN MARK 1:21—3:6

people in ancient times presumed disability to be the result of sin (John 9:2). Furthermore, some sects, notably those at the margins, including the community at Qumran, did consciously marginalize those unable to walk, limiting them from full participation within the collective. Likewise, in the Hebrew scriptures, David, in 2 Sam 5:8, excludes the "lame" from entering the tabernacle; meanwhile, Lev 21:18–19 prohibits those with such a condition from entering the priesthood. In addition to the textual precedent, socio-economic stigma has the potential to develop toward the physically disabled in any culture. Perhaps it was even easier for this to occur in ancient collectivistic societies in which each member was depended on to serve a critical role in the economic stability of the family and community. These factors contribute to Fiensy's model of antiquity's Social Stratification of Persons and Groups, which categorizes the "lame" as among other "expendables," including the unclean.[7]

However, it would be unjust to overgeneralize all of first-century Palestinian Judaism as being excessively harsh to those who are "lame" or disabled, especially since the Hebrew text strongly affirms benevolence in such cases. Additionally, the social view in these situations may well have varied by community. It is notable that Jesus's response in a similar situation in John 9:3 is to say, "Neither this man nor his parents sinned, but he was born blind so that the acts of God may be revealed through what happens to him." Likewise, the scene in this second pericope, Mark 2:1–11, sets the stage for the acts of God to be revealed.

Jesus's Actions

Besides the public setting among a large crowd, the second contrast in Mark 2:1–11 is found in Jesus's words. This man's healing does not appear to be controversial, affirmed by the fact Jesus has healed multiple times already in the Markan text; however, Jesus's words are vital in escalating the scene, injecting a unique healing formula that includes the forgiveness of sins (2:5). Vital to the literary progression is that the question has drifted from an inferred matter of ritual purity that is not considered sinful with the ambiguously identified leper, toward moral purity that does imply sin in the case of the paralytic in this second scene. Nevertheless, the supposed sin or sins are unidentified.

---

7. Fiensy, *Social History of Palestine*, 158.

Jesus's Opponents

Mark 2:1–11 also demonstrates a progression in Jesus's opposition. The critics are specific people in the audience, described as "experts in the law," and they react to the words "are forgiven," words comparable to what a priest might have expressed in Jerusalem. Since Jesus is not a priest, his statement is provocative. The audience is left to consider that perhaps Jesus is insinuating himself to be a spokesman for God, or more strikingly, that he is claiming to have divine authority, as evidenced through the legal experts' thoughts: *"He is blaspheming! Who can forgive sins but God alone?"* (2:7). Nevertheless, this pericope records that they formulate objections in their thoughts, but they do not verbalize the criticism yet. However, the controversy has now escalated since the previous scene. Jesus first touched and cleansed the ritually impure; now, he acts in the authority to forgive sin. The threat increases from a vague hint of danger from unknown enemies in the previous story, to named opponents entertaining specific accusations of blasphemy.

Jesus's Response

In the first pericope, Jesus responds to a vague, unnamed threat through avoidance, leaving town to avoid conflict and continuing his ministry in remote locations. In this second narrative, instead, he publicly confronts the hostile thoughts of his opposition by reasserting his right to forgive sins through a question. He says, "Why are you thinking such things in your hearts? Which is easier, to say to the paralytic, 'Your sins are forgiven,' or to say, 'Stand up, take your stretcher, and walk'?" (2:8–9). He proceeds to heal the paralytic using only his voice through a command to walk. He states that he heals the man "so that you may know that the Son of Man has authority on earth to forgive sins" (2:10), and the result is that "they were all amazed and glorified God" (2:12). Elevated is negative response from some in the crowd, albeit internalized, and Jesus's assertion regarding his own authority to forgive sins.

CHAPTER 3: CONTROVERSY AND RESPONSE IN MARK 1:21—3:6

Pericope 3: Dining with Tax Collectors (Mark 2:13-22)

The Scenario

In the third surveyed passage, Mark 2:13-22, Jesus's interaction with Levi and the tax collectors progresses the variables forward considerably. The setting is public, and the sin addressed is more specific and tangible than in the prior story. The narrative shifts from the forgiveness of one person, the paralytic man, who was culturally presumed to have a sin that remains unidentified, to now incorporate a large group who are of people specifically and obviously identified as sinners by their trade. Moreover, the cultural implications involve accepting and associating with such a marginalized group.

Jesus's Actions

Jesus's actions show an intriguing progression in this passage. His crossing of social boundaries has moved beyond the previous stages of touching and cleansing the ritually impure and pronouncing forgiveness with healing. Here, Jesus accepts hospitality from and engages in table fellowship with Levi and other tax collectors in Levi's home, an interaction which crossed social and religious boundaries.

Social Implications

Mark's inclusion of these toll collectors in 2:13-22 is intended to elevate the stakes considerably. Ancient sources attest to the dishonorableness of their profession, even grouping them with murderers and thieves. Furthermore, their association with gentiles, specifically those linked to the patronage of Rome and Herod, was particularly distasteful and had a widespread perception of being profane. In addition, the action of sharing meals served as a boundary marker in many societies, and within ancient Judaism, table fellowship restrictions were a means of demonstrating who was inside or outside a particular social group. Jesus's table fellowship is an intentional and defiant break from normal cultural engagement with this class of persons, an action linking him with dishonorable characters in a public setting.

As before, one should avoid applying a universal view as a generalization of how all of ancient Judaism viewed sin and purity. However, although this should be navigated carefully, to a cultural sub-group concerned about the threat to the purity of social orifices, the toll collectors represented a great deal of what was wrong in society. If the audience indeed understood these agents to be unclean, as ancient writings suggest, it would not be a stretch to conclude that they viewed the tax collectors as morally impure as well. They operated as legal bandits dealing with coins bearing the Roman image, which could amount to idolatry, especially given the royal imperial cult that worshiped Caesar as a god. According to the most dramatic viewpoint, these "sinners" would have incurred infractions at all levels, ritually, ethically, and morally, with perhaps their primary social stigma stemming from being collaborators to occupying forces.

Jesus's Opponents

The response of Jesus's adversaries again progresses in this story. It moves beyond internal, mental dialogue to verbalized criticism; however, a subtle nuance remains in that they do not directly confront Jesus with their questions, but rather his disciples. Moreover, unlike the previous scene in with a single concern was contested, namely the forgiveness of sins and blasphemy, this section identifies a double concern—Jesus's ethics of table fellowship as well his avoidance of fasting (2:18–22). This spoken criticism is a clear escalation among the opposition, but again, it is not voiced to Jesus directly, nor is a specific disagreement labeled.

Jesus's Response

Jesus's reaction also escalates. He progresses from responding via a question in the previous pericope, asking, "Which is easier?" (2:9), to a clear assertion in this passage. Referring to the tax collectors and sinners, he says, "Those who are healthy don't need a physician, but those who are sick do. I have not come to call the righteous, but sinners" (2:17). Here he has added the descriptor of Physician to sinners to the previously stated title of Son of Man. His opponents reiterate a challenge regarding fasting as another means of discrediting his shared meal with the tax collectors, and Jesus responds a second time, justifying his methods with a triple parabolic affirmation. First, he referring to himself as the bridegroom; then states old garments cannot be patched with new cloth because they will shrink and pull; and, finally, asserts that old wineskins cannot accommodate new wine or both will be destroyed; instead, they require new wineskins (2:18, 22). All of these imply that the socially marginalized are more receptive to Jesus's mission than the religious elite.

Pericope 4: The Sabbath (Mark 2:23—3:6)

The Scenario

The final section from Mark 2:23 to 3:6 incorporates two portions comprising a double Sabbath controversy. Such a "back-to-back" scene itself progresses the series of escalations. Interestingly, whereas the first two pericopes involve healing and the third involves food, this double controversy scene incorporates both food and healing. These compounded sections take place on the Sabbath, with the final setting in the synagogue in Capernaum (2:2, 3:3). Interestingly, this location, a synagogue, is identical to the venue at the beginning of Jesus's ministry in Mark 1:21 (in the synagogue in Capernaum on the Sabbath), which is accompanied by the pronouncement, "he taught them like one who had authority, not like the experts in the law" in 1:22. Then, the text in 3:3 says, "Then Jesus entered the synagogue *again*" (emphasis mine), revisiting the prior setting and recalling those words at the outset of his ministry.

Social Implications

The Sabbath was one of the most critical Jewish identity markers. As noted by James Edwards, "Sabbath is not simply another article of faith in Judaism ... [but a] defining characteristic ... even more than circumcision, [it] determined one as an observant Jew."[8] Once more, the entirety of Judaism is not represented by the presentation of Jesus's opponents. Sub-societies such as the Essenes prohibited certain humanitarian efforts on the Sabbath, but this hardly creates a generalization applicable to the entire population. Furthermore, as Craig Keener attests, "no sect in early Judaism had rules that would have mandated Jesus's death for his Sabbath practices."[9] However, in the Second Temple period, certainly during Roman occupation, this primary identity marker became a crucial public preserver of Jewishness, again reinforcing boundaries of the body politic.

8. Edwards, *Gospel according to Luke*, 176.
9. Keener, *Matthew*, 462.

Jesus's Actions

Mark presents Jesus and his group crossing socio-religious boundaries, specifically in the eyes of some Pharisees. This double-Sabbath escalation initially involves food, like the previous passage; however, as the disciples pluck the grains of corn, the issue is no longer a mere failure to exercise the dietary discipline observed by the fasting Pharisees on any given day. Now, the lack of discipline is compounded because the infraction occurs on the Sabbath. Jesus makes a comparison between his group's actions and David's entourage consuming the bread reserved for priests. If Jesus's earlier language in the healing of the paralyzed man is a bit more subtle, resembling a priest's pronouncement of forgiveness of sins and using the phrase "Son of Man," now the comparison to David presents an escalation.

Jesus's Opponents

On the first of the two Sabbath occasions, Jesus's opponents finally issue an objection to him directly. However, their approach is still nuanced, expressing concerns only about his disciple's behavior, saying, "Look, why are they doing what is against the law on the Sabbath?" (2:24). However, by the time of the second Sabbath scene, the opponents are intentionally preparing a trap, finally ready and waiting to confront Jesus. The text reports that they "watched Jesus closely . . . so that they could accuse him" (3:2). However, stymied by Jesus's question and riposte regarding the true nature of good and evil on the Sabbath, they elect instead to remain quiet, but have by no means given up. His adversaries finally form an unlikely partnership with the Herodians in a plan to execute Jesus. This is the most serious opposition he has faced.

Jesus's Response

In this double Sabbath scene, Jesus delivers the greatest assertion of his authority. In the first Sabbath scene, he escalates his authority by comparing himself to David, and then asserting, "The Sabbath was made for people, not people for the Sabbath. For this reason, the Son of Man is lord even of the Sabbath" (2:27–28). Then, in the next scene, he shows that he is Lord of the Sabbath through question and riposte and a tangible demonstration. Jesus preempts the Pharisees' attempt to accuse him by asking the question, "Is it

CHAPTER 3: CONTROVERSY AND RESPONSE IN MARK 1:21—3:6

lawful to do good on the Sabbath, or evil, to save a life or destroy it?" (3:4). Jesus then commands the man with the withered hand to stretch out that hand, again healing with a word rather than a touch, reminiscent of his command for the paralytic to get up and walk, which also recalls his authority to forgive sin. Ironically, the Pharisees had implicated Jesus as being guilty of associating with socially exiled groups; yet they themselves plot with the unclean Herodians to do evil and destroy life, on the Sabbath, no less, while Jesus is the one who has done good and restored health and life on the Sabbath. The observation regarding their plotting answers Jesus's questions for the audience—these individuals are the ones whose actions are evil.

Synthesis

The literary progression of conflict in these four episodes demonstrates Jesus's increasing authority, as well as the danger he faces. Religious and socio-cultural dilemmas comprise the first level of increasing intensity. The first scene addresses the boundary of ritual impurity and the healing skin diseases, in which no sin is explicit. The subsequent scene escalates by involving the forgiveness of implied sin. The third dilemma allows for table fellowship with the morally profane, who, significantly, are indirectly Roman and/or Herodian operatives. Finally, in the double Sabbath narratives, the author addresses and redefines the topic of defiling the Sabbath.

Jesus's perceived risk levels in his boundary-crossing also increase in intensity. In the first scene, Jesus could have been considered polluted through contact with the man with skin disease, but he also could have remedied this through purity rites. In the second scene, the announcement of pardon for sins is riskier. It does not necessarily mean Jesus is marking himself as divine, but it could mean he is identifying himself as a prophet or as having the authority of a priest. This stretches propriety even more. In the third story, Jesus characterizes his table fellowship in the context of a doctor treating the sick, although the tax collectors were repulsive sinners in the minds of many first-century listeners. Finally, the accusation of Sabbath violations could have seemed inexcusable to some, as noted by the repetition; and in addition, Jesus's self-identification as "Lord of the Sabbath" is much closer to blasphemy than his announcing forgiveness of sins, or even his self-comparison to David. Jesus is implied to have sinned himself through violating the sanctity of the Sabbath, a cardinal institution of Jewish identity.

Accordingly, the reaction of Jesus's opponents also escalates. Initially, both his enemies and the threat against him are unnamed, involving only a vague sense of danger. In the next scenario, his enemies are identifiable, described as experts in the law (2:6), and their criticism takes the form of internalized thoughts. In the third sequence, his adversaries are named as experts in the law and Pharisees (2:17), and they openly question Jesus's disciples. In the final double Sabbath scene, his opponents are Pharisees (2:24, 3:7), and they progress from questioning Jesus concerning his disciples' behavior to finally forming direct accusations against him and seeking to kill him. This escalation sequence is a critical foundational piece for the author of this Gospel. Mark's audience is to know that while Jesus does not *really* break the Sabbath, his opponents hold him in suspicion for doing so. Such an accusation has now moved beyond the scope of ritual purity, the forgiveness of sin, and table fellowship with a marginalized group associated with moral profanity to engage in a controversy focused on the Sabbath being defiled. Each of these are critical of socio-cultural Jewish identity markers of increasing importance in society.

The final aspect of the author's literary progression takes the form of increasing assertions and demonstrations that build on each other and establish Jesus's identity. Previously, the text has shown him to be one who teaches with authority (1:22), one who casts out unclean spirits (1:27, 34, 39) and one who heals (1:30–31, 34). Now, in this series of four pericopes, first, he cleanses impurity (1:41–42); second, he proclaims himself the Son of Man who has authority on earth to forgive sins (2:1–11); third, he describes himself as the Physician of sinners (2:16–17), and the bridegroom who pours new wine into new wineskins (2:18–22); and fourth, he identifies himself with David, reasserts that he is the Son of Man, and describes himself as the Lord of the Sabbath. Each pericope is like an arrow pointing the direction toward the next to reveal and justify who Jesus is. As Jesus's identity, power, and ethics are increasingly legitimized, likewise, the religious leaders are first subtly and then blatantly revealed to be the villainous characters of the story. The progression of the pericopes builds tension for the final outcome of Jesus's story.

Opportunities for Further Research

This chapter articulates an enhanced view of Dewey's literary connection, taking her work describing this unity and drawing out further literary components. Of the Synoptic Gospels, Matthew, while retaining each of these accounts, has interrupted the Markan order, thus eliminating this literary progression of intensifying encounters. On the other hand, even though Luke redacts the material, he maintains and prioritizes the Markan order in Luke 5:12—6:11. The redactions serve to generate a smoother reading, enabling these stories to be read as even more closely aligned and preserving the increasing tension and revelation of this unit of stories. This chapter's findings highlight the reasonable expectation that the Lukan inclusion of the Markan order is intentionally based on preserving a clear literary progression.

Luke's inclusion of the Markan order could potentially be connected to Luke's emphasis on ministry to the marginalized and gentiles, through which the mission of Jesus is developed via these progressive controversial scenes depicting attention to societal outcasts. However, there are secondary options that might be considered in Luke's retention of the Markan order, including the supposed anti-Semitism of Luke-Acts or the eschatological temple and new priesthood theology as examples. Regardless, this study builds a foundation for future research for those who wish to consider the progressive nature of this Markan sequence in light of its adaptation in the Synoptic Gospels.

Chapter 4: A Galilean Peasant's Reception
"The Prodigal Son" in the Context of Luke's Travel Narrative, a Social-Scientific Reading

WHEN READING SCRIPTURE WITH Western eyes, cultural bias is unavoidably imposed upon the text. There is no better example of this than in Jesus's parables, particularly those with some economic function.[1] To many Westerners, rugged individualism is seen as a virtue, contrary to the world of the text in which community is valued. Furthermore, the freedom of choice, pursuit of happiness, and even the sacredness of capitalism are staples of the world's foremost individualistic societies such as the United States of America. However, when reading the parable of the prodigal son (Luke 15:11–32) from a Western perspective, readers will inevitably miss the socio-economic dilemma caused by the younger son's insistence on a financial enterprise of individuality.

The remarkable works of Richard Rohrbaugh and Kenneth Bailey each offer unique but credible insights into cultural elements of the New Testament texts. Leaning on and adding to these scholars' contributions, this chapter's purpose is to generate a socio-historical reading of Luke 15:11–32 reflecting the worldview of the Bible, thereby shedding light on Luke's intended themes and underlying purpose in the parable of the prodigal son.

---

1. This study was originally presented at the Eastern Region Annual Meeting of the Evangelical Theological Society (virtual) April 9, 2021, themed "Misreading Scripture with Western Eyes."

CHAPTER 4: A GALILEAN PEASANT'S RECEPTION

An Initial Reading of the Parable

A Disordered Household

Middle Eastern readers immediately recognize the disorder of the household when the first voice is not of the senior character, but that of the younger son (15:12).[2] This disorder is magnified by the father's compliance with the son's request (15:12). Furthermore, the elder son's early inactivity automatically raises alarms, given the cultural expectations for him to have served in mediation on such an occasion.[3] The father is the most mentioned character of this parable, and his judgments are the most concerning, especially within a patriarchal society.[4] The father grants not only the premature inheritance, but also the unthinkable privilege to liquidate the property (15:13).[5]

Selling Ancestral Land

In the world of the text, typical inheritance was comprised of real estate and the assets held on that land; meanwhile, cash assets were at a minimum. Therefore, this younger son would have had to sell property to secure money. The sale represents the younger son's rejection of his genealogy; and now that the family has lost one third of the estate, their annual income would be significant reduced, diminishing their economic security.[6] With a lone son now at home, the family was also more vulnerable should the elder son suffer the common fate of short life expectancy, leaving the family without legal protection. In collectivistic societies, the community also suffers, since the example of the younger son could establish a precedent, potentially prompting similar action by other sons.[7] The family would be viewed as having shamefully defied social expectations, and the community would likely distance themselves from this family.[8]

---

2. Bailey, *Finding the Lost*, 112.
3. Bailey, *Finding the Lost*, 122.
4. Bailey, *Finding the Lost*, 114.
5. Rohrbaugh, *New Testament in Cross-Cultural Perspective*, 94–95.
6. Rohrbaugh, *New Testament in Cross-Cultural Perspective*, 98.
7. Rohrbaugh, *New Testament in Cross-Cultural Perspective*, 92–93.
8. Rohrbaugh, *New Testament in Cross-Cultural Perspective*, 97.

Villagers would have refrained from purchasing land from the family, sold by the younger son, wishing to avoid contributing to this household's shameful behavior.[9] Therefore, the younger son would have sold his portion to an outsider unconcerned with community perception.[10] By necessity, such a land transaction would have taken place unusually fast, sold at under its value.[11] Essentially, the younger son needed to leave the village expediently before suffering the wrath of the community; therefore, he would have sold with an urgency that benefited the purchaser.[12]

The Younger Son

The younger son's mismanagement of wealth and excessive living is compounded by a famine, leaving him to pursue a foreign benefactor who grants him the vocation of tending pigs (15:13–15). In Middle Eastern culture, the polite way to reject a potential client is to give them a duty they will not accept.[13] However, the younger son is desperate to fulfill even a detestable task such as this (15:16). After having rejected his own family, the younger son, now hungry and without community in his newfound land, decides to return home (15:17–19).

The Patriarch

When the father sees the younger son, he shamefully runs to meet him, a sign of a patriarch being out of control (15:20). However, unruly behavior is consistent with every aspect observed from this household. This reunion is on full display for the village within collectivistic life. The younger son fails to deliver the rehearsed speech in entirety; now recognizing his inability to bring honor to the family after seeing his father's shameful action before the community.

The father demands the robe and ring to be quickly brought to the younger son, communicating his restoration of sonship to the village

---

9. Rohrbaugh, "Peasants, Widows, Bandits."
10. Rohrbaugh, "Peasants, Widows, Bandits."
11. Rohrbaugh, "Peasants, Widows, Bandits."
12. Rohrbaugh, "Peasants, Widows, Bandits."
13. Bailey, *Finding the Lost*, 126.

before the son can suffer their wrath (15:22–24).[14] Meat was not routinely eaten, and beef was reserved for occasions requiring a significant amount of people since they could not refrigerate the excess meat once a large animal was butchered. However, the father must satisfy the village by hosting a banquet for restitution.

The Elder Son

Attention turns to the elder son, who is the second son making his way home to meet the father outside the house that day. Upon hearing the party, the elder son ascertains that the younger son was received with *hygiaino*, or peace, and becomes angry, refusing to enter the gathering, disrespecting the father and village guests (15:25–28). This shame is increasingly magnified when the father leaves the party guests to negotiate with the elder son (15:28–32). In doing so, the father lowers himself from the status of family patriarch to that of an equal with the elder son. The elder son insults the father by addressing him without the proper title before shaming himself while rejecting his proper role both as a host and an elder son, instead identifying as a servant or more accurately a slave (15:29). Both sons have forced themselves into a voluntary exile.

Reflections on Economic Status

An Economically Privileged Household

Having concluded the initial reading, this study will now briefly argue that the father's household was among those of the economically privileged. The trajectory of land ownership in first-century Palestine favored the wealthy, while many peasants succumbed to debt obligations. A minority of the population owned the majority of the land. To have an estate large enough to divide was increasingly unique.

Second, after losing a third of the estate due to the younger son's liquidation, the narrative gives no indication that this family has lost significant economic status. The text indicates the father maintained both slaves and craftsman, as well as the fatted calf (15:17–23). Furthermore, the younger son remarks that the craftsmen have excess bread, establishing them in a better-off category than the widespread subsistence-living

---

14. Bailey, *Finding the Lost*, 152.

populace (15:17). Next, Joel Green argues that, even with the reduced land, the elder son manages employees and slaves on family land distant enough to have not been aware of the events surrounding the younger's return, indicating extensive land holdings.[15] Finally, Craig Keener attests that the ring placed on the younger son's finger was another indication of the economic well-being of the household.[16]

A Peasant Audience's Reception

The parable, while directed to the Pharisees (Luke 15:1–2), was also presumably heard by a widespread peasant audience. The prodigal son is not unlike other parables of Jesus in that its implications would differ from the perspective of peasant listeners than from those of higher status.

To a peasant audience, the land transaction in this story represented everything wrong in society. Hearing of an economically stable outsider taking advantage of a desperate seller, a peasant audience would have had images of the wealthy urbanites exploiting the debt system that had foreclosed on much property among the peasant population. Furthermore, these land patrons were not only outsiders, but were despised city people, sometimes even Roman citizens, representing outside control. It would have also seemed repulsive for the younger son to voluntarily relinquish his land to go to the city, of all places.

Second, a peasant audience would have felt more vindication than sympathy for the son who used his money unwisely, thus suffering hunger during a famine and sinking to the depths of feeding pigs. Essentially, the view would have been that the wealthy should get what they deserve, suffering as they have made others suffer. Many peasants faced hunger, as well as the shame of losing ancestral land and being exiled. Upon the younger son's return, a peasant audience would have been disappointed that he did not get his "comeuppance" by having to face the wrath of the village. Furthermore, the father's reception would be designed to provoke anger in this audience, who would see no lasting consequences for the younger son's foolishness. The father's wealth covers the mistakes that peasants cannot afford to make. Even though the younger son lost it all, to both the peasant audience and the elder son, it feels like his situation was restored; simply put, the rich get away with anything.

15. Green, *Gospel of Luke*, 584.
16. Keener, *IVP Bible Background Commentary*, 222.

Next, the elder son is ungrateful, a detestable quality in Mediterranean life, especially so to peasants observing this attribute among the wealthy. The elder son's greed is more apparent when it is affirmed that although he retains his full inheritance, the loss of a calf still provokes hostility. The elder brother even slanders his younger counterpart, which could have had serious consequences if taken as a credible scenario. However, to the audience in the world of the Bible, it is plain to see that the entire family has been foolish; both brothers are greedy, and the father is undignified, and yet they hardly seem to experience lasting economic repercussions.

The Village in the Parable

In a collectivistic world, one must ask how this greed affected the peasant village. In honor-shame cultures, people fear being made a mockery of. After the village solidarity had been threatened, these peasants attended the father's banquet, and it appears they, like the younger son, were willing to do so under the motivation of their hunger. The rich have bought off the peasant population through their bellies, making a mockery of them. Most likely, the reception of this parable is equally difficult to the peasants as it is to the Pharisees, but for different reasons. To a peasant audience in the ancient world, the outcome of the parable is scandalous. Rather than perceiving the parable as conveying theological truths depicting a father's generous love, they would more likely have received the idea of grace as a societal injustice, which would tend to unsettle and disturb such a populace. Rohrbaugh's work on this parable also calls attention to the fact that the city was a fatal attraction to many peasants who end up with failed ambitions of financial success;[17] and ironically, the core section of Luke's Gospel (9:51—19:27) is unmistakably a narrative in which Jesus, a peasant, is on his way to the city (Luke 9:51).

Implications

Parables of the Wealthy in Luke

The parable of the prodigal son exhibits similarities with other stories told during the travel narrative to Jerusalem—the good Samaritan (Luke 10:25–37), involving elitist priests and Levites who are disconnected from

---

17. Rohrbaugh, *New Testament in Cross-Cultural Perspective*, 99.

the peasants' realities; the parable of the rich fool (Luke 12:13–21), told in response to two brothers arguing over inheritance; the excessiveness of the rich man and his neglect toward Lazarus (Luke 16:19–31); and the rich ruler, who seeks to maintain his wealth (Luke 18:18–30).

Then, the rich ruler is juxtaposed with Zacchaeus (Luke 19:1–11), whom Darrell Bock, without elaborating, describes as a type of the prodigal son.[18] Zacchaeus's parallel to the younger brother in the prodigal son is better understood when viewed in conjunction with the rich ruler (Luke 18:18–30) as a type of the elder brother. Both the rich ruler and the elder brother claim to be commandment-keepers, but are diminished by their covetousness.

In the stories of Zacchaeus and the rich ruler, as with the elder and younger brothers in Luke 15:11–32, all the characters are men of means, and each one has exhibited greed. However, Zacchaeus, like the younger son of Luke 15:11–32, is eventually rescued from his shame and finds community through a process of separation from possessions. The positive outcome for Zacchaeus and the younger brother contrasts with the failure of multiple other wealthy characters in Luke. These include the elder brother of Luke 15:11–32, the rich ruler of Luke 18:18–30, the rich man of Luke 16:19–31, the rich fool of Luke 12:13–21, and even the priest and Levite of Luke 10:30–35, who are all to some extent examples of the failures of self-reliant individualism.

The Parable as the Central Point in Luke

The parable of Luke 15:11–32 leaves the reader to grapple with deeper implications regarding the author's intent. In typical fashion, just as Luke designs the Jerusalem Council to be the center point of Acts, the author designs the center of the Gospel of Luke to contain a pivotal narrative with the parable of the prodigal son. First, throughout his ministry, Jesus gathers a group of exiled prodigals; and some of them, like the younger son, motivated by their physical needs, in Luke's extended travel narrative are making their way to Jerusalem, the center of socio-religious life. Meanwhile, having gathered this community, Jesus, among other things, is rebutting societal greed; and when he reaches Jerusalem, the first thing he does is to enter the temple, identifying the greed associated with the institution (Luke 19:45–46).

18. Bock, *Luke*, 2:1896.

CHAPTER 4: A GALILEAN PEASANT'S RECEPTION

Broader Themes and Unanswered Questions

N. T. Wright correctly observes in this parable a broader theme of return from exile, and remarks that to many Jews, a return from exile had never fully occurred. The Jewish community remained in need of full restoration, in large part due to economics; they were enormously in debt, most of their ancestral lands remained lost, and foreign occupiers ruled them politically and economically.[19] Ken Bailey notes that aspects of the parable resemble Messianic language wherein, by experiencing shame, the father becomes a suffering servant bringing his family to restoration.[20] Jesus is depicted through a character humbling himself to become exalted, taking a path toward shame to later reunite a family in Jerusalem.

To the frustration of some, the final reaction of the elder brother remains unknown. A repetitive question in Luke's travel narrative becomes increasingly more explicit: How will the "elder brothers" of Jerusalem, who never "sinned" or left home, receive their exiled counterparts when Luke's extensive travel narrative meets its conclusion? Will they identify their arrival as a moment to revive the community? Will the Judeans accept a teacher from among their Galilean "younger brothers"? How would they respond to a reinstitution of community whereby the definition of neighborliness even extends to exiled Samaritans? The father received the younger son with *hygiaino*, a Greek counterpart to the Hebrew *shalom*—peace. How will Jerusalem—the city of peace—receive Jesus with his exiled younger brothers? As with other portions of Luke's travel narrative, the author leaves the story open-ended, designed to evoke self-reflection in the audience.

---

19. Wright, *Jesus and the Victory of God*, 176–79.
20. Bailey, *Finding the Lost*, 173.

Chapter 5: A Social-Scientific Analysis of Simon the Magician's Request in Acts 8

Introduction

THROUGHOUT LUKE-ACTS, STATUS AND wealth are portrayed with disdain; meanwhile, the call to relinquish money and possessions, resulting in a lowered social position, is a critical component of discipleship.[1] However, Simon Magus is an unusual character whose participation in the life of the *ecclesia* is rejected even though he has expressed the intent to surrender money and to serve the church in a critical (but inappropriate) role. This study will take a two-part approach—first, examining critical elements of Acts 8:4–24; and second, applying socio-scientific interpretation to this text, applying concepts such as patronage, limited good, and honor challenges.

Observations from the Text

The Samaritan Mission

The events leading up to Acts 8:4–24 offer insight into understanding this passage. In the preceding section, following the martyrdom of Stephen, Saul's persecution prompts a gospel diaspora (Acts 7:54—8:3). Philip is the one who carries the Messianic message to a *polis* in Samaria, fulfilling Jesus's commission in Acts 1:8, saying, "you will receive power when the Holy Spirit has come upon you, and you will be my witnesses in Jerusalem, and in all Judea and Samaria, and to the farthest parts of the earth." The Samaritan reception of the message is described in a way that is

---

1. This topic was first presented as a paper read at the British New Testament Society annual meeting on Saturday, August 21, 2021, at University of St. Andrews, Scotland.

intentionally indicative of the mission's success; the crowd is *homothumadon* ("in one accord"), echoing the description of the one hundred twenty in the upper room in Acts 1:14. In Acts 8:6, the Samaritans are observed hearing and seeing (*akouō* and *blepō*), two vibrant theological concepts in Luke-Acts. The unclean spirits are driven out of the community (8:7), and healing is received (8:7), thus prompting great joy (8:8), another sacred expression in Luke-Acts. Here, Luke creates a narrative contrast between the affirmed Samaritan response and the disposition in Jerusalem, represented by the ruling elite, which has resisted the church and is growing more united in its opposition.

Introducing Simon Magus

Simon's character is then introduced using repetitive language in 8:9–11. He is twice described as a practitioner of "magic" (*mageuō*), and twice as having "captivated" (*existēmi*) these Samaritans. The word "great" (*megas*) is used three times in quick succession, becoming a signpost for reading this pericope. Simon knew himself to be great, which is also acknowledged by the Samaritans. Those from the greatest to least in society pay Simon attention (*prosechō*), a word also used to describe their response to Philip. Perhaps most significantly, Simon is identified by the populace as being the "power of god" (*dynamis ho theos*).

Magic and Power

Magic, within this context, is about the control of people and forces. In the ancient context, magic is rooted in a view in which all beings, natural, supernatural, demons, and divinities alike, could be influenced or manipulated by certain rituals. Therefore, magic was generally viewed as being a component of religion, not necessarily its antithesis. The purpose of magic was to counter problems in public and private life. Examples include the protection from spirits and sickness or to assist in successful ambitions. The concepts of good and evil magic were determined by the effects of the practice on society.

Power, like magic, is also theological in Luke-Acts, with overlapping characteristics. Power is the ability to control others, and it generates honor for its holders. Richard Horsley substitutes terminology for miracles, magic, and exorcisms, calling them simply "acts of power," applied to Jesus when he confronted spiritual, social, religious, and political forces, thus attesting that the core struggle is against the powers that controlled the people.[2]

Simon vs. Philip

Magicians like Simon enjoyed large followings. In an honor-shame society, since honor, specially acquired, is subject to the court of public opinion, Simon's status signifies that he had an honor claim, which indicates that his deeds served to benefit the population to some degree. Furthermore, Simon appears in at least a divine mediatory role, given his title of the "power of god" (8:10).

Acts 8:12 clarifies that Philip preached the gospel correctly, specifically the kingdom of God, in the name of Jesus Christ. Upon the Samaritans' expression of faith (*pisteuō*), they were baptized (8:12). Simon was no exception, coming to faith (*pisteuō*), and was baptized in parallel to the crowd (8:13). Therefore, to outright dismiss Simon's conversion simultaneously casts suspicion on Philip, who presumably baptizes him after assessing something genuine.

Both Simon and Philip displayed their abilities before the Samaritan *polis*, performing mighty deeds and giving oral proclamation while receiving careful attention from the people. Simon is known as the "great power" (8:10); meanwhile, Philip works "great miracles" (8:13). Simon likely saw himself in a capacity similar to that of Philip, and due to his existing honor status, the populace may have shared this perception. However, a reversal occurs once Simon is "amazed" by Philip and no longer amazes the community (8:13).

Peter and John

The arrival of Peter and John adds authority to authenticate the Samaritan response and validate Philip's work (8:14–17). The apostles pray for the Samaritans to receive the Holy Spirit and then lay hands on them, seemingly transmitting the gift by this method. The world of the text viewed the laying on of hands as exerting force and as an activity of transference; therefore, this appeared to be the formula of Holy Spirit impartation. Simon assesses this as the method and proposes an exchange of money for the apostolic

---

2. Horsley, *Jesus and the Powers*, 2–3.

gifts (8:18–19). It was common in Greco-Roman society to give monetary donations as a gateway to entering the priesthood, for example.

Peter responds by cursing Simon—"May you and your silver be destroyed" (8:20)—asserting the failure of rationalizing that gifts reserved for apostolic deployment could be received via barter. Peter then urges Simon to repent and pray for forgiveness, accusing him of corruptness of heart (8:21) and of being in the "gall of bitterness" and "chains of unrighteousness" (8:23).

Simon's Position

At this point, Simon must limit his shame by agreeing with his superior, a social requirement in ancient Mediterranean life. Simon recognizes Peter to be a divine broker, able to speak curses and to mediate forgiveness and favor. He requests that Peter pray for him to avoid realizing the curse (8:24). What Mitzi Smith calls Simon's "humble" response should be more accurately categorized as desperate.[3] The curse of which Simon was a victim was viewed to be a serious threat.

Some might suggest that Simon provokes the sympathy of the reader. The intrigue of this narrative is compounded by the mystery regarding its outcome. Some deduce that this account serves as an ongoing warning of challenges faced by all disciples, specifically the use of money and consumer goods.

Socio-Historical Deductions regarding Simon Magus

Having examined the text, it is helpful to eliminate one interpretive possibility. While one can presume that Simon's source of money comes from his former profession as a magician, the method through which he obtained the money does not directly influence Peter's rejection of Simon's proposition. In Luke's Gospel, Jesus visits the homes of tax collectors (Luke 5:29–30, 15:1–2, 19:1–10) and accepts their hospitality, even though it has been made possible by exploitation. The source of wealth is therefore not a deterrent from fellowship.

---

3. Smith, "Acts," commentary on Acts 8:24.

However, this study presents seven intriguing interpretive proposals drawn from a socio-historical viewpoint that provide a deeper understanding of the dynamics at play in this text.

Patronage Relationships[4]

The first proposal is that Simon's honor had been acquired from a patronage relationship with the client Samaritans. In a world where honor and dishonor comprised the fundamental social values in society, the text reiterates Simon's greatness and parallels him to Philip. Simon captivated members of all socio-economic status in this *polis*, inferring that he held a prominent seat among the social hierarchy. Without any evidence of his honor being ascribed or inherited, Simon's honor claim would have been achieved through his practiced magic, through which, in exchange for money and honor, he granted requests. This type of relationship cemented a patronage bond between the two parties. The patron-client relationship was not based on socio-economic equality but rather on asymmetrical reciprocity, by exchanging different kinds of goods. Patronage was not only an expected reality in the ancient world but also a necessity in a society where power rested in the hands of the few. However, once he engaged in this relationship, Simon's honor and wealth depended on the magician continuing his deeds to maintain the clients who needed him.

This patron-client theory, as applied to Simon, is not without nuance. For example, Simon could be viewed as functioning in the role of a broker more than a patron. If indeed, as some contend, his clients accepted that Simon served in a mediatory role between a deity and the population, his honor would still have theoretically been no less than that of Philip, Peter, and John as brokers of the gospel. Brokerage was an essential vocation used to gain acquired honor, especially for those serving in a mediatory or priesthood role between divine patrons and their client humans.

---

4. Patronage relationships in the ancient world is developed more extensively in chapter 10 of this volume, entitled "Father, Son, and Spirit: Symbols of Patronage and Reciprocity in Luke-Acts."

CHAPTER 5: SIMON THE MAGICIAN'S REQUEST IN ACTS 8

Limited Good[5]

Second, this study proposes that Simon perceived the Holy Spirit as being in finite supply in the limited good society of the ancient world.[6] Modern industrial nations tend to think of an expanding economy in terms of expected periodical cost-of-living wage increases. However, this mindset contrasts with the worldview of Luke-Acts. The people in the world of the Bible saw themselves as being controlled by nature while living a heavily taxed, greatly indebted, and largely agrarian life, whereby everything was in great demand and short supply. This concept of limited good supply transferred beyond agriculture, wealth, land, and all areas of economics into every facet of life, including health, beauty, procreation, honor, social status, food, water, and so on. Essentially, the concept of limited goods implies a zero-sum game, whereby the supply cannot increase. This social construct creates elevated levels of competition, since each success, gift, or blessing afforded to a person is perceived to deplete the overall supply for others; hence, the resource bank for goods becomes limited, with society fearing its eventual elimination.

Given these cultural dynamics, all goods were viewed as being in limited supply, including the Holy Spirit. This perception would have seemed to be justified by the initial incomplete experience of the Spirit at Philip's preaching, which was later made complete by the apostolic visit by Peter and John. From the perspective of the new Samaritan believers, apparently, the supply of the Holy Spirit was limited enough that not only Simon, but also Philip, the gospel broker, would be excluded from apostolic participation in distributing the Spirit. Furthermore, the newfound faith in Jesus by the Samaritan *polis* meant that Simon's honor status had been depleted in a zero-sum environment. The limited good he previously offered, his magic, is no longer in demand; therefore, he must quickly and desperately attempt to rebuild his honor. Hence, if Simon is to have a chance to control another limited good such as the Holy Spirit, he must make his appeal quickly while that resource remains in supply. In that society, typically the community power brokers would expect to use a resource such as this to exploit others and earn income.

---

5. The topic of the Holy Spirit as a limited good is also developed in chapter 10, "Father, Son, and Spirit: Symbols of Patronage and Reciprocity in Luke-Acts."

6. Neyrey, "Limited Good," 103.

This proposal in turn generates numerous other theological assertions and questions. For instance, commentators discuss Peter's clause "if possible" (8:22) regarding Simon's potential to repent. When framed from the limited good perspective, a relevant question becomes whether Peter believed that forgiveness could also be a commodity in limited supply.

Simon's Envy and Shame

The third proposal asserts that as Simon strived to regain his honor position, his envy was revealed, a detestable quality. Philip's gospel presentation was confirmed by signs, including the driving out of evil powers. Simon ceased his practice of magic, although the reason is unknown. Did Philip's exorcisms and other manifestations of power render Simon impotent? Were his services no longer needed because what Philip provided was free of charge? Or did Simon voluntarily relinquish this power? The answer is unknown; regardless, the result is that Simon has now lost the means for his honor claim among the community, which were the source of not only his status but also his income. Simon's motive is evident in his offer to exchange money for the apostolic gift. One prevalent signpost early in this text was Simon's greatness, which has now been lost. Simon's remedy is to retrieve his worth to the *polis* by becoming a broker to transmit the Holy Spirit. In doing so, he would maintain a position whereby he could continue to serve the client population at will. Due to the perception of limited goods, Simon may have presumed that the populace would need continual transmissions from a broker.

In a limited good society, jealousy in terms of the desire to maintain honor status is expected and could be considered akin to virtue. However, what Simon desires is not merely to maintain his own honor status, but to rival the status of Peter and John, genuine apostles of power and patrons or very high-level brokers of the *ecclesia*.

In contrast to the virtue of jealousy, envy, or desiring what someone else had, was a disreputable quality. Simon's proposal amounts to envy—not only seeking what others had (in this case, the apostolic gifts), but also reaching for an honor claim that far surpasses his status, that of an apostle.

Furthermore, this desire is further tarnished because, in a limited good society which is a zero-sum environment, an increase in honor status for one person suggests that another will be deprived. In Simon's case, for an unworthy recipient to receive apostolic gifts would imply that someone worthy of the calling might in turn be excluded from those gifts.

In the world of the text, honor was a passion for those who desired success. It was the principle that motivated all conduct in one's life. In Simon's quest to replenish his honor, he instead became the recipient of shame. This shameful status is not only limited to his position in the newly established church fellowship, but it is also on full display to the general community, which has grown to see him now as a deviant rather than as a prominent member of society. Simon's social reversal is complete; indeed, the first is becoming last. Simply put, Simon's jealousy over regaining his honor status would have been acceptable; however, the envy over others with the gift of laying on of hands was shameful.

An Honor Challenge

The fourth proposal is that Simon's actions amounted to an honor challenge, one which was won by Peter. Honor challenges were common in the first-century Mediterranean world. In fact, any public interaction offered the potential to enhance or diminish personal honor. Therefore, many types of exchanges, including business proposals, could qualify as honor challenges.

Simon's proposition indicates that he sees himself as worthy of utilizing apostolic gifts; however, Peter appears to be insulted, seeing Simon as corrupt and unable to match him on the honor scale of the *ecclesia*. Luke has already crafted Simon's status in parallel to Philip's early in the narrative; therefore, it is not inconceivable that an honor challenge would ensue. Furthermore, if Simon's primary motives are to recapture his quickly eroding honor, the best way to achieve this would be to become the victor of an honor challenge with the apostles. At work here is a battle of indispensability. In the ancient Mediterranean world, vocation was akin to identity. Simon had become dispensable, and now his proposal threatens the indispensability of Peter. When viewed in this context, this is a classic honor challenge.

For this to be an honor challenge, Peter would be expected to offer a riposte. Furthermore, a meaningful way to assert one's honor status was in the mastery of language, including what Pilch calls the "art of insult."[7] Peter's stark language to Simon demonstrates a suitable mastery of language

---

7. Pilch, *Cultural Handbook of the Bible*, 161.

and a certain win in this challenge. He combines insult with threads of theological language to curse Simon, to the extent that the former magician offers submission rather than rebuttal, thus relinquishing the honor claim to his opponent rather than shaming himself even further.

Simon's Motivation

The fifth proposal is that Simon's position within the community and his proposition to the apostles is rooted in his desire for power, control, and exploitation. The contrast is evident: Simon, while losing his honor status, still retains whatever wealth he has accumulated. At best, this is indicative of a disciple who is not fully committed in the context of Luke-Acts. Simon likely still has more substantial wealth than Peter and John; therefore, this gave him the basis for a modest honor claim, and his honor would surge higher than ever if he succeeds at securing the apostolic gifts. Thus, as Simon has benefited from the power or control as a patron of people in the past, he attempts to do the same with the apostles, gaining control over them with offers of money just as he influenced spirits with magic. If this passage is understood as portraying an unconverted Simon, then to him, the Holy Spirit would appear to be superior magic that he intends to utilize through the means of continued control and profit.

The world of Luke-Acts was one of economic exploitation, with a wealthy few taking advantage of the vast majority living at or near subsistence levels through a variety of means. This included the credit markets, whereby failure to pay the enormous principal and interest rates would result in the seizure of land, assets, and the rendering of persons into slavery. A reading where Simon represents this type of artistry of manipulation is likely a valid one.

Richard Horsley formulates a view, leaning on Mark's Gospel but also interacting with Luke, that exorcism was associated with resisting the power in control—namely, Roman domination, which would also incorporate the idea of resisting political brokers who exploited the majority population.[8] Some of Horsley's conclusions may be overstated, but this reading of Luke's Gospel has merit—for example, when considered in the context of Jesus's testing in Luke 4:1–13, when he rejects the offer of the devil's patronage to grant him power over kingdoms. This is an example of Luke's association of imperial power with the dark powers.

8. Horsley, *Jesus and the Powers*, 121–30.

CHAPTER 5: SIMON THE MAGICIAN'S REQUEST IN ACTS 8

Horsley's theory becomes a worthwhile template for examining Simon, who was evidently in a power broker position within this Samaritan *polis*, but who had lost his influence after the exorcisms that accompanied Philip's arrival. Nothing from the text definitively indicated that Simon used his powers in an exploitative way; however, it can be inferred based on the political and economic realities and the control he likely exerted as a patron. One key indication is that the author identifies Simon as a magician rather than a miracle worker, which carries some stigma of greedy behavior compared to perceived benevolence of the latter. Therefore, it is possible that Simon could be representative of any exploitative powers, including that of empire.

A Kin Group Outsider

Proposal six is that Simon further alienated himself from the church by insulting its unique polity. The early ecclesiastical structure is that of a kin group. Luke-Acts employs an extensive volume of kinship language. One hallmark of kinship is that group behavior within the family was distinct from interactions with those outside the family. In other words, if one treated someone from the kin group as an outsider, this would be a mark of shame. For Simon, his proposal of a relationship based on patronage was an insult to the structure of the *ecclesia*, where, similar to a household, members held all things in common. Furthermore, a basis of kin group functions was uniformity in terms of goals and ambitions, ideally void of competitiveness. However, it seems that Simon did not accept this model, since it would require him to accept his lower social status and intermingle on near equal terms with his former clients. Rather, he elects to engage in competitive behavior.

Purity Boundaries

The final and seventh proposal is that Luke-Acts reconstitutes purity boundaries, and that Simon broke two primary identification markers of cleanliness. The concept of purity comingles with honor and shame as a method of governing human behavior. Purity denotes who is clean and pure, as opposed to the defiled and polluted, essentially identifying who is appropriately marked as part of the in-group. Additionally, purity markers identify those at the margins or outside of the group's boundaries, and they signal inconsistent group behavior. Purity standards are a way of enforcing group ethics, placing each person on a map according to position and compliance.

In Luke-Acts, some traditional purity markers are consistently challenged; meanwhile, the newly evoked standard of cleanliness is rooted in new economic and social ethics. Furthermore, given the group's orientation as a collectivistic culture, it was expected both in society and especially within the church that individuals would forsake their personal preferences for the common good. Simon fails this purity test. Rather than laying possessions at the apostles' feet for the common good, he attempts to bribe them; and rather than being willing to surrender his honor, humble himself, and conform to the ecclesiastical model of kinship, he tries to rewrite the ecclesial model into one of secular patronage in order to benefit himself and enhance his honor.

This is one reason why it was necessary for Peter to give a sharp response, even at the expense of Simon's reputation. Through his answer to Simon, Peter intentionally constructs a distinct boundary between the power of God and pagan rituals and indicates clear purity markers of the movement. In doing so, Peter references Isa 58:6. In context, this immediately follows a rebuttal articulating the futility of religious exercise without humility by those who fulfill their selfish desires by oppressing workers (Isa 58:3–7). Then, following, the text prescribes sharing food with the hungry, shelter for the homeless and oppressed persons, and clothing to the naked (Isa 58:7–10). Luke's John the Baptizer is unique in duplicating this formula, which became the identity marker of the church in Acts (Luke 3:10–14). Here, Peter highlights the contrast between the "all things in common" (Acts 2:44, 4:32) disciple group and the selfish exploits intended by Simon, the failing disciple. If discipleship prompts Zacchaeus, another Lukan character, to offer half his assets and repay exploitation at a 400 percent rate (Luke 19:1–10), then what might be required of Simon?

Was Simon Converted?

At the conclusion of this narrative, the question goes unanswered of whether the account of Simon is the first mention of a named individual conversion in Acts, or merely an example of what conversion is not. Admittedly, from a theological and literary point of view, it would be odd for this occasion to present the first instance of a conversion of a named person. The following pericope, that of the Ethiopian eunuch, presents a less controversial and more theologically vibrant case of conversion (Acts 8:24–40), and its literary position creates the possibility that the alignment of the two pericopes is intended to contrast a failed conversion with a true one.

Furthermore, the only other apparent occasion in Luke-Acts describing a gift being rejected takes place in the context of Jesus's honor challenge in Luke 4:1–13, in which the patron devil offers Jesus a brokerage role that would give him authority over the kingdoms of the world in exchange for worshiping him. That dark comparison does not aid in making a case for Simon's authentic faith. In the contest between Peter and Simon, Peter is offered money rather than political authority, and he likewise passes the test offering inappropriate patronage and reciprocity.

Simon's story bears some resemblance to the plotting and greed of Ananias and Sapphira in Acts 5:1–11. However, the contrast is that Simon is given a chance to live and repent. Some speculate that Simon was more ignorant than Ananias, thus less accountable. The reality that Peter opened the door for repentance should not be overlooked. While it could be viewed as indicative of in-group behavior, since forgiveness, patience, and reconciliation were values of kinship, it could also be that Ananias and Sapphira's fate was the result of in-group behavior, while the exchange with Simon was milder because it was an outsider interaction.

Synthesis

The case of Simon's precise status as a Christ-follower remains a mystery. He falls somewhere between the rich ruler of Luke 18:18–24, who is disturbed and retreats due to the implications of discipleship toward wealth and honor, and Zacchaeus of Luke 19:1–10, who relinquishes possessions, makes restitution, and is affirmed as a true son of Abraham. Peter opens the door for repentance, but the account does not convey what happens next. What is certain from this account is that Simon has transitioned from being admired for his greatness among the entire social strata of his community, to becoming dispensable, a terrible status in the ancient world. This causes him to lose his honor claim as a magician, to shamefully display his envy, and to publicly lose an honor challenge to Peter. Through the account of Simon Magus, Luke conveys the theological truth of Jesus's teaching that "those who exalt themselves will be humbled" (Luke 14:11).

Chapter 6: Election and Divine Sovereignty in Acts 8:26—10:48 in Relation to the Gentile Mission

Introduction

THE BOOK OF ACTS records the development of the early church, including the progression of salvation history, especially to the gentiles. At the beginning of Acts, in a massive communal event following Peter's preaching in Jerusalem at Pentecost (Acts 2:14–40), three thousand respondents are baptized (Acts 2:41). In addition, in the adjacent scene after Peter's presentation at the temple in Jerusalem (Acts 3:11–26), an additional five thousand persons responded positively to his message (Acts 4:4). Moreover, although the focus early on in Acts remains on the Jerusalem ministry following the negative events associated with Ananias and Sapphira (Acts 5:1–11), the narrator provides commentary that many joyfully receive the apostolic message, without specifying how many (Acts 5:14). Luke also notes that a substantial number of priests have come to faith in Jesus (Acts 6:7).

Up to this point in Acts, the author has identified those who receive the good news and profess faith in Jesus in a collectivistic context with individual anonymity. However, although reception of faith by masses of people occurs throughout the book, the author relays three noteworthy individual encounters in Acts 8, 9, and 10. Given the author's narrative intentionality, the attentive and detailed callings of the Ethiopian (Acts 8:26–40), Saul of Tarsus (Acts 9:1–31), and Cornelius (Acts 10:1–48) serve to accentuate that these are landmark occurrences. These events are significant within soteriological history, highlighting divine sovereignty in the personal election in these events as a means of legitimizing the mission to the gentiles.

CHAPTER 6: ELECTION AND DIVINE SOVEREIGNTY IN ACTS 8:26—10:48

The Ethiopian Eunuch (Acts 8:26–40)

The context surrounding this encounter sheds light regarding the author's intent in describing the eunuch's calling. Prior to this passage, following the persecution prompted by Stephen's stoning, the church begins to spread beyond Jerusalem. It makes its way to Samaria through Philip's preaching (Acts 8:4–13), and when the Samaritans prove to be receptive to the apostolic message, Philip calls for Peter and John to come and provide a specific endorsement of the activity in the region. This enables these new believers to receive the Holy Spirit (Acts 8:14–25). Part of the significance of the event is that the Jesus movement has now spread from Jerusalem to Samaria, a location long divided and marginalized from the Jewish temple cult due to the Jewish perception of the Samaritans as an ethnically mixed people. While Acts 8:4–25 does not directly convey that God intervenes to direct the church toward Samaria, God's direction is inferred since this occasion fulfils Jesus's words of Acts 1:8, that the message would spread even to Samaria and the "ends of the earth" (Acts 1:8). Undeniably, the diaspora (Acts 1:1–3) of persecuted Christians fulfills that mandate.

Following the Samaritan scenario, the author records an event more explicitly directed by God. Philip receives specific instructions from an "angel of the Lord" to travel (Acts 8:26) and, simultaneously, a eunuch who serves a prominent role for the queen of Ethiopia is traveling the same road. The eunuch's initial faith status is debatable, but he appears to have some devotion to Jewish practice, evidenced by his reading of Scripture and observation of a religious ritual in Jerusalem (Acts 8:27). The Holy Spirit guides Philip toward this Ethiopian's chariot (Acts 8:29) where Philip recognizes that the individual is reading the Isaianic text but is unable to understand a considerable portion of the writings (Acts 8:28–31). (Interestingly, while the Ethiopian is reading regarding the Messiah in Isa 53:7–8, not much further along in the text, he is bound to encounter the passage in Isa 56:3–7 directed toward eunuchs.)[1] Philip responds to the man by articulating the good news of the events associated with Jesus. The narrative manifestly demonstrates that this encounter alters the eunuch's experience

---

1. "The eunuch should not say, 'Look, I am like a dried-up tree.' ... For the eunuchs who ... choose what pleases me and are faithful to my covenant ... [and] foreigners who become followers of the LORD and serve him, who love the name of the LORD and want to be his servants ... I will make them happy in the temple where people pray to me ... for my temple will be known as a temple where all nations may pray."

and produces his baptism; and subsequently, immediately, the Spirit escorts Philip away (Acts 8:32–40).

The plain reading of this text reveals that this encounter between Philip and the Ethiopian is not mere coincidence but is divinely designed and orchestrated, placing each party in a precise location at an appointed time. First, Philip had been told by the Lord's messenger to travel in a specific direction, lacking any indication that his route would intersect with the eunuch. Second, although Philip had likely encountered many travelers, the Spirit explicitly informs Philip to direct his attention to the eunuch. Third, the timing is so precise that the Ethiopian was reading the Messianic text of Isa 53 at the moment of the encounter, requiring assistance to understand the passage. Moreover, the encounter occurs close to a source of water, facilitating the baptism. Finally, to confirm God's absolute control over the circumstance, Philip is supernaturally transported elsewhere at the conclusion of this encounter.

Scholarship affirms the divine orchestration of this meeting. F. F. Bruce acknowledges that "divine guidance" is vividly recorded in the instruction to Philip,[2] and I. Howard Marshall remarks that this entire scene was "instigated by God," evidenced by the fact that the Spirit's presence in this text is "overruling what happens."[3] Meanwhile, Mitzi J. Smith remarks that "every aspect of the meeting between Philip and the Ethiopian is divinely orchestrated."[4] Joseph Fitzmyer affirms that from the onset of the story, the clear indication is that the events that surround this narrative are "God-inspired."[5] This encounter presents an intriguing issue of narrative importance given that the Ethiopian eunuch is the first individual remarked upon who is baptized in Acts.

Saul of Tarsus (Acts 9:1–31)

Saul is introduced at the stoning of Stephen. The author notes that the cloaks of the participants are placed at his feet (Acts 7:58), an antithetical image recalling Barnabas and other church members placing money at the feet of the apostles (Acts 4:35, 37). Saul intends to travel to Damascus to arrest Christians (Acts 9:1–2); however, his journey is interrupted by an

---

2. Bruce, *Book of the Acts*, 174.
3. Marshall, *Acts*, 170.
4. Smith, "Acts," commentary on Acts 8:26–40.
5. Fitzmyer, *Acts of the Apostles*, 411.

CHAPTER 6: ELECTION AND DIVINE SOVEREIGNTY IN ACTS 8:26—10:48

intense light accompanied by the voice of Jesus (Acts 9:3–5). Meanwhile, in Damascus, a disciple named Ananias receives instruction from God through a vision informing him to wait for Saul, whose destiny is to carry the message of Christ while suffering for the cause (Acts 9:10–15). Ananias is obedient to the command. He finds Saul at the location directed by the Lord, and he lays hands on Saul, whose vision is restored, and who then receives the Holy Spirit and is baptized (Acts 9:16–19). Saul's response is to quickly begin proclaiming Jesus at the synagogues, leaving people surprised at his sudden reversal from persecutor to proponent of the Jesus mission (Acts 9:20–22). In the same chapter, Saul avoids a plot against his life and makes his way to Jerusalem to the apostles (Acts 9:23–25).

Marshall notes that in this narrative, the bright light with the accompanying voice are both signs of a divine revelation and are the basis for Paul's later affirmation that he had met the risen Jesus.[6] Hans Conzelmann remarks that while Saul's companions were present and aware of the voice, the revelation came to Saul alone, not to his traveling partners, which further supports God's deliberate action in election and calling of a specific person at a particular occasion.[7] Plenty of debate has ensued over the last half century over whether the nature of Saul's revelation in Acts 9 is a calling or conversion. Although this nuance rests beyond the scope of this project,[8] in either case, the experience is the moment that John Reumann correctly describes marking "the great reversal in Paul's life because of the risen Christ."[9]

In the Damascus Road narrative in Acts 9, the providence of God is on full display. The Lord determines a specific person to call to accomplish a particular task while first granting him the grace of a remarkable revelatory experience. In this, God's initiative and sovereignty are revealed in addition to a vocational predestination for the emerging Saul. Furthermore, God's deliberate placement of Ananias to perform his will provides further testament to divine involvement. Perhaps equally striking is that Saul's companions on his journey presumably do not receive any revelatory message

---

6. Marshall, *Acts*, 178.

7. Conzelmann, *Acts of the Apostles*, 58.

8. The project intentionally sidesteps conversion language as it at times is anachronistic. Moreover, the Samaritans and, even to a debated or lesser extent, the Ethiopian, Saul, and Cornelius are all in one way or another already sympathizers with Judaism at the very least, to a pious observer at the other extreme. This purpose of this chapter is to discuss election as a vocation and function rather than personal soteriology.

9. Reumann, *Philippians*, 516.

whatsoever. The author's intention is assuredly to depict God's election of Saul and his sovereignty over Paul's mission.

Cornelius (Acts 10:1–48)

The narrative tied to Cornelius, a Roman centurion, represents the third time the Lukan author describes a personal instance of election and divine sovereignty. At the outset, Cornelius experiences a vision of an angel during his prayers who specifically instructs him about locating Simon Peter (Acts 10:1–8). The following day, God's intervention is evident concerning Peter, who falls into a trance and sees a vision that guides him to eat creatures unclean according to Judaism. Almost immediately following this vision, Cornelius's messengers arrive, requesting that Peter accompany them back to the centurion's home (Acts 10:9–23). Upon his arrival, Peter remarks that although Jews are normally forbidden to be inside the home of an unclean gentile, Peter understands because of his vision that it is God's will for this rule to be superseded (Acts 10:28). Likewise, Cornelius relays his vision, in which Simon Peter recognizes a confirmation of God's new work in opening the gospel to the gentiles. While Peter proceeds to tell Cornelius and his household about Jesus, the Holy Spirit comes upon his listeners, and they are baptized (Acts 10:30–47). The story concludes in chapter 11 with Peter's reiteration of this story upon his return to Jerusalem, reconfirming God's blessing on this gentile centurion and his family.

Unquestionably, the events of Acts 10 are anything but random, exhibiting multiple instances of God's handiwork. Nearly simultaneous visions are visited upon two vastly different individuals in distinct locations. That this opportunity was extended to and received by Cornelius is only possible through God's design.[10] These visions from God serve to connect these two men despite improbable and even taboo circumstances. Their connection serves as a bridge between what has thus far been predominantly a Jewish apostolic mission in early Acts and the subsequent broader-reaching, gentile-inclusive Pauline ministry.

---

10. Cornelius's story represents the mostly likely example of a circumstance involving what could be termed a conversion, given that he is obviously a gentile; however, Luke presents him as being in the "God-fearer" category of one who already has respect for God.

CHAPTER 6: ELECTION AND DIVINE SOVEREIGNTY IN ACTS 8:26—10:48

Other Instances of Sovereignty

Unquestionably, Luke seeks to convey that the critical events of the early church do not occur by accident, but rather rest within the will of God as a fulfillment of divine actions. These three occasions are far from the only instances in Acts that evidence God's providence. A survey of just the first five chapters demonstrates several other occasions that reinforce God's sovereignty at work. For example, in Acts 1:24, the apostles depend on providence in the selection of Judas's replacement; Acts 2:47 lends support to God's sovereignty in election; and in Acts 5:38–39, Gamaliel asserts that if the movement is of God, it will survive, which is a direct inference pointing to God's sovereignty.

Synthesis

Each of the three accounts shares similar features building the author's support for the argument of God's sovereignty within the election of each person. In all three passages, persons, places, and timing were divinely orchestrated. Three times in a row, the author describes an event that requires two parties to have heard from God simultaneously, and the final story is reiterated twice for even more emphasis. Although the reception of faith by masses of people occurs throughout Acts, these three instances are recorded as extraordinary occurrences given their significance within salvation history.

According to the Old Testament, the Ethiopian's status as eunuch designated him unable to enjoy first-class participation in Judaism. Yet, this less-than-second-class citizen has now received salvation and the Holy Spirit without prejudice through a sovereign process. In the next instance, Saul, formerly a persecutor of the movement, becomes the primary apostle to carry the message of the gospel to the gentile world. The record of his reception demonstrates God's endorsement of his apostolic mission. Finally, Cornelius's acceptance of the message provides additional evidence of God's unfolding plan to extend his covenant to the gentiles by way of this divinely intended salvation experience. This was accomplished through God's sovereignty working through Peter, the primary apostle of Acts up to this point. Therefore, each of these encounters is tied to what may be considered a "policy change" from an exclusively Judaic movement to the inclusive nature of the Jesus movement in the developing early church.

The question of whether these encounters demonstrate full conversion/s remains uncertain and perhaps anachronistic. Each of these persons required a dramatic and overwhelming shift to become full beneficiaries of God's grace at work in the early church. However, a more likely explanation of these stories' inclusion is that Luke prefers to use clear acts of providence to demonstrate when a story marker or narrative shift happens.

The events with the Ethiopian eunuch distinctly evidence that those within his category, the formerly excluded eunuchs, are candidates for full participation within the emerging Christian movement. This narrative, in terms of God's sovereign actions through Philip, echoes the Samaritan account just preceding it wherein the apostolic endorsement by Peter and John was necessary to convincingly articulate that the happenings in Samaria are in alignment with divine will. Likewise, the critical encounter with the Ethiopian, also potentially controversial, is also filled with evidence of God's sovereignty, creating a compelling argument that the inclusionary shift was indeed God-ordained.

Moreover, in the case of Saul of Tarsus, the evidence of God's providence is overwhelming. His personal posture dramatically changes, reallocating his interests from the persecution of the Jesus movement to evangelism on its behalf. His subsequent important mission to gentile-dominated regions where non-Jewish converts would become critical components of the movement also becomes a clear attestation of God's will, reflected by this sovereign calling. Such a narrative shift is consistent with Saul's later dream regarding the Macedonian man (Acts 16:9–10), which likewise is intended as a literary signpost of the expansion of the early Christian movement from Asia Minor into Greece (modern Asia to Europe), reflected by God's clear orchestration of the event.

Moreover, with Cornelius, his gentile status compounded by his role as a centurion is potentially controversial. However, as the key transition begins in Acts toward the gentile inclusion, Cornelius presents one of the gentile mission's first test cases. The remarkable circumstances also point to a clear exhibition that God's sovereignty commanded the events, reiterating that this considerable inclusion is divinely decreed.

Conclusion

Having considered three major instances of personal transformation wherein God's sovereign actions are irrefutably articulated, this study can

CHAPTER 6: ELECTION AND DIVINE SOVEREIGNTY IN ACTS 8:26—10:48

consider the following proposition as a closing hypothesis. The narratives concerning the Ethiopian, Saul of Tarsus, and Cornelius do not require an outright conversion experience, as each is indicated to have some prior awareness of and devotion to God. Most likely the reasons their callings are presented with unique detail signaling divine orchestration is that their election into the church signifies that significant boundary markers are being expanded.

The bookended characters represent surrogates. The Ethiopian depicts the mission to Africa, which is not a primary concern for Luke, either due to his predominant interest in the Roman destination or his lack of material from the African context. Nevertheless, the eunuch serves to indicate that the gentile mission will fulfill the mandate to the "ends of the earth" (Acts 1:8). While this character's ethnicity is a key factor, his genital status also represents an imperative ideological expansion.

Likewise, the centurion serves as a representation of gentiles in general, especially in the Mediterranean. Like the Ethiopian, Cornelius incorporates a secondary but vibrant quality in that his imperial responsibilities complicate and enhance his character, indicating further expansive qualities in the gentile mission.

In crafting the story of Paul, the central of the three characters, Luke wishes to express and authenticate the apostle's Jewish credentials and divine election, which is necessary since Paul will be the primary agent carrying the mission to the gentiles and the furthest reaches of the Roman empire and, significantly, to the city of Rome itself.

While some speculate that Luke's interest in developing these three characters via divine sovereignty is to describe their salvation or conversion, it is most likely that Luke's objective was to demonstrate providence in their election, which functions as archetypal relations to their demographics or missional perspectives. This invites further avenues of scholarly exploration, specifically, but not limited to, how sovereign election might function in other parts of Luke and Acts, more specifically the latter, especially in relation to the gentile mission. Additionally, one might consider how these characters may be an ideal disciple within the Lukan corpus, or even more, an ideal witness to others in apostolic church. The relationship between these characters and others, Sergius Paulus, a Roman politician as Paul's first convert for an immediate example in Acts 13:4–12, might yield fruitful results.

Chapter 7: Luke's Progressive Revelation of Jesus's Identity—Son of God, King, and Christ

Introduction

SCHOLARSHIP HAS ENGAGED WITH limitations Luke's use of the titles "son of God," "king," and "Christ," throughout Luke-Acts; however, few have considered the robust progression of these terms and how Luke layers their deployment. Moreover, although Jesus's identity is articulated to the reader of the Gospel early in the account by way of the angelic and prophetic oracles in Luke 1–2, Luke unfolds the public revelation of Jesus's identity in a nuanced way. This chapter considers how the author uses questions and assertions of Jesus's identity to foreshadow and then unfold his identity as Son of God, king, and Christ throughout Luke-Acts.

Questions of Jesus's Identity

Although Luke 1–2 outlines Jesus's identity, which is known to specific individuals including Mary (1:30–38), Elizabeth (1:42–45), the shepherds of Bethlehem (2:8–14), Simeon (2:25–32), and Anna (2:36–38), his identity is concealed from the public as evidenced in post-infancy. However, Luke's literary style presents an unveiling of this identity in the public sphere through a progression of questions.

The initial inquiry is made by Jesus to his mother, who, at least in part, seems somewhat unaware of the full import of the circumstances in Luke 2:46–50. Jesus amazes his audience with questions, leaving his mother perplexed when he asks her a question directly relating to sonship.

CHAPTER 7: LUKE'S PROGRESSIVE REVELATION OF JESUS'S IDENTITY

Luke 2:48 recounts Mary's remark to Jesus, "Your father and I have been . . . looking for you," while Jesus redirects with a question "Why were you looking for me? Didn't you know that I must be in my Father's house?" (2:49). While Mary is attentive in Luke 1–2 to the events surrounding her and delivers prophetic oracles herself, Jesus's question indicates that more is to be revealed, even to Mary.

The mystery of Jesus's identity continues as chapters 3 and 4 unfold. When John the Baptist is introduced in Luke 3:1–22, the people question whether he might be the Christ; however, John, deflecting their question, redirects them elsewhere without directly revealing the identity of the one whom he proclaims (3:15–16). Even the subsequent baptism of Jesus with the accompanying voice from heaven appears limited in its conveyance to the general public regard for Jesus's identity (3:22). The scene in the next chapter generates more questions regarding Jesus's identity (4:1–13) when the devil questions Jesus's legitimacy, stating, "if you are the Son of God" (4:3, 9). In the literary progression, Jesus's identity remains under question not only in that wilderness scene, but also in his hometown of Nazareth when they ask, "Is this not Joseph's son?" (4:22). Again, while readers are provided with the keys to Jesus's identity early on, the characters in the text continue to seek clarity, including the man with a demon in Capernaum who also proposes a question, saying, "Have you come to destroy us?" (4:34).

The questions continue to develop in chapter 5 when the public gathers to pay attention to Jesus. He heals a man unable to walk, marked by the forgiveness of sins (5:20), which prompts the question "Who is this man . . . who can forgive sins but God alone?" (5:21). In the adjacent scene, questions of Jesus's identity are not asked directly, but are certainly inferred by the Pharisees and lawyers, who ask the disciples, "Why do you eat and drink with tax collectors and sinners?" (5:30). The inference to matters of identity is, to some extent, recognized by Jesus when he responds by likening himself to a physician (5:31).

The expectation builds as the controversies and questions continue in chapters 6 and 7. When Jesus heals on the Sabbath and is asked, "Why are you doing what against the law?" (6:2), he proceeds to unveil another aspect of his identity, describing himself as "lord of the Sabbath" (6:5). The narratives concerning identity continue as John the Baptist requests his disciples to approach Jesus, asking, "Are you the one who is to come, or should we look for another?" (7:19). Jesus responds by clarifying John the Baptist's identity, stating that of "those born of women no one is greater than John" (7:28). However, to the reader, Jesus's explanation is also embedded within his own Christology, as he is clearly greater than John the Baptist. In the infancy narratives, the comparisons and contrasts between the birth announcements of John the Baptist (1:12–17) and Jesus (1:30–38) describe the latter with greater superlative.[1] Moreover, in Luke 7:27, Jesus declares John the Baptist's fulfillment of prophecy. The implications highlight that the greatness of John must be exceeded by the one for whom he prepares the way. Accordingly, these remarks, via questions, layer additional revelation to Jesus's identity.

The question of Jesus's identity builds and peaks in chapters 8 and 9. First, Jesus demonstrates the power to quiet the storm (8:22–25), provoking the disciples to ask the question, "Who then is this?" (8:25). Finally, as the conclusion to the Galilean ministry approaches, Jesus confronts his disciples twice in a row with pointed questions concerning his own identity. He asks, "Who do the crowds say that I am?" (9:18) compounded by "Who do you say that I am?" (9:20). Up to this point, the narrative tension has continued to build throughout Jesus's public ministry concerning his identity, specifically in Galilee. The culminating feature that prompts the conclusions of the questioning motif of Jesus's ministry occurs in Galilee, when Jesus solicits Peter's positive affirmation in response, "the Christ of God" (9:20). Following these pointed questions, the literary trajectory changes and shifts toward Jerusalem (9:51), and these types of question then largely cease, perhaps revisited to limited extent during his trials in Jerusalem.

Progression of Key Term: Son of God

The description of Jesus as "Son of God" builds in a subtle but progressive way throughout the text of Luke-Acts. The introductory material of Jesus's life in the Lukan Gospel conveys to the reader that Jesus is the Son of God through Gabriel's message to Mary (1:32, 36). Still, to the public, as with other aspects of Jesus's identity, this remains an unfolding mystery in Luke's literary progression. The narrative moves from the angel's remark to Mary to the pronouncement of God himself at Jesus's baptism that "this is my son" (3:22). The next voice to speak to this sonship is another spiritual force, the devil, who raises the question of Jesus's sonship to God. Without precisely affirming it, the devil is plainly aware of this status (4:3, 4:9). As

1. Just, *Luke 1:1—9:50*, 62.

CHAPTER 7: LUKE'S PROGRESSIVE REVELATION OF JESUS'S IDENTITY

with the term *Christ*, in the beginning of the Gospel, only spiritual forces apply this expression to Jesus.

The narrative progresses by eliciting questions about Jesus's sonship. The next remark regarding sonship occurs in Jesus's hometown of Nazareth when the people ask, "Is this not Joseph's son?" (4:22). However, ironically, although people in Nazareth did not recognize Jesus's true identity, as reflected by their question of sonship, he is acknowledged with high honor in Capernaum, where Jesus enjoys more success. The first human voice affirms Jesus's divine Sonship, albeit through the demonic inspiration, saying "you are the Son of God" (4:41). This demonic affirmation is echoed in Luke 8:28 when a demon implores: "leave me alone, Jesus, Son of the Most High God." In chapter 9, Jesus's Sonship is again expressed, this time by God at the transfiguration scene, stating, "This is my Son, my Chosen One. Listen to him!" (9:35). Through Jesus's Galilean ministry, only spiritual forces, God, Gabriel, the devil, and demons refer to divine Sonship. In the subsequent portion of the Gospel, Luke's travel narrative (9:51—19:27), the only time the subject is raised is in 10:22 when Jesus affirms that "no one knows who the Son is except the Father."

In the final portion of the Gospel, in Jerusalem, the first and only mention of Sonship is at Jesus's trial (22:70). The chief priests and teachers of the law ask him, "Are you the Son of God, then?" However, while this priestly human voice raises the question, rather than seeking to affirm this standing, it seeks to find an excuse to execute Jesus for making such claims. This is only time that Sonship is raised by a human in the Gospel, other than Jesus's oblique reference or the human who was possessed by a demon. However, even though the demons utter strong affirm of Jesus's Sonship, it is telling that the priesthood only seeks to make a mockery of it. This is the final occurrence in which the Gospel of Luke mentions divine Sonship. In the entire Gospel, the appellation never occurs unless it is under the clear direction of a strong spiritual influence, as to this point it has only been remarked upon by God, Gabriel, the devil, demons, and Jesus himself. This allows speculation whether the author intends the reference by the priesthood to symbolize that the priesthood is under the influence of supernatural forces.

In contrast, in Acts, for the first and only times, Jesus is referred to directly as the Son of God by a human voice that affirms this relationship as truth. The one to affirm this trait is Saul of Tarsus, who upon his interruption on the Damascus Road begins to immediately proclaim Jesus as the Son of God (Acts 9:20). Paul later expounds upon this as a fulfillment of Ps 2 in Acts 13:33. Curiously, Saul of Tarsus, otherwise known as Paul, is the only human voice giving affirmation to Jesus as the son of God; and the author uses the phrase only these two times in the entire book of Acts.

Progression of Key Term: King

In addition to Jesus's Sonship, Luke progressively develops the idea of Jesus as King. Jesus is connected to the kingdom of God, both prophetically in Luke's introductory material and practically as he would proclaim this kingdom. However, the development of kingship is a bit more subtle. Luke presents Jesus as King, but in a way that also progresses in its literary development. It is not until Jesus enters Jerusalem that kingship language is applied. This occurs when the crowds recite from Ps 118:26, "blessed is the king who comes in the name of the Lord." However, Luke has injected the word "king" here into the context, since the Psalm uses a pronoun rather than the word "king" in Luke 19:38. Then, during his trial, Jesus is accused of and questioned about his status of kingship although he does not directly respond (Luke 23:2–3). Subsequently, at his crucifixion, Jesus is mocked by the soldiers saying, "if you are king of the Jews, save yourself" and by the inscription "this is the king of the Jews" on the cross (23:37–38).

Up to this point, the volume of hints concerning Jesus's kingship have taken place largely via questions and mockery, but not through an outright conclusive affirmation in the text other than the imposed insertion into the 118th Psalm quoted by the crowd. However, the first direct affirmation given to Jesus's kingship from a human voice originates from the criminal beside him at his execution who petitions, "Jesus, remember me when you come into your kingdom" (Luke 23:42). Therefore, the author's literary development is such that not until the final moments of this Gospel is Jesus declared directly, by any voice, to be King; and that occurrence takes place through an unexpected source.

Interestingly in Acts, while the "kingdom of God" language is recorded, on no occasion do the apostles likewise refer to Jesus as a king. The sole evidence of any hint of Jesus as King takes place in Acts 17, when, in Thessalonica, Paul and his companions are driven out of town being accused of proclaiming a king other than Caesar, namely, Jesus (Acts 17:7). However, in this case the author does not reveal any details of Paul's preaching that would have led to this accusation.

CHAPTER 7: LUKE'S PROGRESSIVE REVELATION OF JESUS'S IDENTITY

Progression of Key Term: Christ

The Petrine affirmation of Jesus being "the Christ" (Luke 9:20) presents a segue into discovering how the author develops the term *Christ*, as applied to Jesus, in the literary progression of Luke-Acts. The initial occasion referencing Jesus as Christ occurs in the angels' announcements to shepherds (Luke 2:11), which is reaffirmed through the experience of Simeon by the Holy Spirit (2:26). The crowds question whether John the Baptist might be the Christ since the people remains uncertain (3:15); however, even though the public is undecided, the demons Jesus casts out "knew that he was the Christ" (4:41), although they do not speak the word and are forbidden to do so. From these accounts, it is apparent early in Luke's Gospel that spiritual forces, both angels and demons, are aware of Jesus's Christological attributes, in addition to Simeon to whom it is revealed by the Holy Spirit, and the shepherds who receive word by means of the angels. However, not until chapter 9 does a human voice ever confirm this reality based on personal realization with Peter's affirmation of Jesus's being the Christ, although this occurs in a limited public setting (Luke 9:20).

Following Peter's recognition of Jesus as the Christ, the term is absent during the entire travel narrative to Jerusalem (Luke 9:51—19:27). The word is not mentioned again until it is raised by Jesus's accusers who place him on trial, but never does anyone call him that title except in mockery (Luke 23:2, 23:35, 23:39). Only at the conclusion of the Gospel does the post-resurrection Jesus, speaking in third person, affirm himself to be Christ for the first time in the Gospel, in chapter 24 (24:26, 46).

In comparison, the book of Acts is saturated with the use of this description. The early church in Acts attributes the title of Christ to Jesus so frequently that his name becomes attached to the title to form the appellation "Jesus Christ" (Acts 2:38, 3:6, 4:10, 8:12, 9:34, 10:36, 10:48, 11:17, 15:26, 16:18, 24:24, 28:31). Furthermore, in Acts, Jesus being Christ is the foundation of the proclaimed message (Acts 2:31, 2:36, 3:18, 4:26, 5:42, 8:5, 9:22). The usage of this term was so widespread that Luke records the transition in which the early believers become formally recognized as "Christians" sometime after the gospel made its way outside Palestine to Antioch (Acts 11:27).

The term *Christ* is a sensitive, blatant, and highly charged attribute in the historical setting of the Gospel. It is used with such a great reserve in the book of Luke that it seems that it must intentionally be kept a secret throughout the narrative, just as Jesus instructs the demons in Luke

4:41, and it is only self-affirmed by Jesus at the culmination of the Gospel. However, once Jesus identifies himself as the Christ, the term explodes with frequency in Acts. The contrast is so great that the author must have designed this to be so. Just as the author uses the literary technique of question and response to gradually reveal Jesus's identity, the word *Christ* serves as the final, potent "reveal" of who Jesus is. While Jesus frequently self-identifies as the "Son of Man" in Luke's Gospel, that third person reference to himself as Christ is the only occasion during which he attributes the phrases "Son of God," "King," or "Christ" to himself in Luke's Gospel. The importance of this revelation bursting on the scene sets the stage for establishing the identity of the early church, and, likely, that is why that title was prioritized in the early church proclamation. Building the narrative this way seems intended to justify the gospel message and the believers' self-designation as followers of Christ.

Conclusion

Luke's word choices and literary design are deliberate. The author clearly spends a great deal of effort developing Jesus's identity. This is especially true of his identification as the Christ. The author reveals this slowly yet deliberately via a literary progression, often implementing a process of sincere human affirmation and proclamation as well as question and response. In contrast, the affirmation of Jesus's Sonship, while present, is sparing, and the affirmation of Jesus as King is minimal compared to the declaration of the kingdom of God or Jesus as the Christ.

Tracing the progression of these terms is only the beginning of the potential that such a study might offer. The relevant question for future development is what Luke's motivations and purposes might be, especially in the instances where he redacts Markan material. Some initial theorizations might be presumed true, yet are hardly explored in scholarship, presenting opportunity for further engagement. For example, the title of "king" is a politically charged term, as is "son of God" and even "Christ." The book of Acts demonstrates how "king" becomes problematic at politically strategic locations like Thessalonica (Acts 17); hence, the title is used with reserve. However, "son of God" and "Christ" are also potentially problematic, the former being a title devoted to Caesar himself, and the latter being ascribed to multiple individuals exhibiting Jewish revolutionary messianic tendencies. Despite this, "Christ" is used

CHAPTER 7: LUKE'S PROGRESSIVE REVELATION OF JESUS'S IDENTITY

pervasively in Acts after the "secret is out," so to speak, possibly because of Luke's interest in Jesus fulfilling Jewish tradition.

These ideas invite a segue into further exploration, as some argue that Luke was writing for the purposes of a political apology for the Roman imperial authorities. Additional concepts regarding questions of Jesus's identity remain undeveloped, and these also warrant further notice, including additional titles uniquely employed by Luke, such as Jesus's self-designation as "Son of Man," or the Davidic connection including Jesus as "son of David" in Luke-Acts. Moreover, other areas of potentially fruitful research are in why Luke prioritizes Jesus's Galilean ministry as the grounds to establishing his identity (1:1-9:51), while the material in the travel narrative is largely absent of these features (9:51—19:27). Lastly, Luke's selection of specific characters who make particular affirmation offer a curious research possibility. These questions regarding Jesus's identity remain undeveloped but warrant further examination.

Chapter 8: Deuteronomic History and the Portrayal of Solomon in Luke-Acts[1]

Introduction

THE LUKAN TEXTS ARE firmly rooted within the language, style, and prophetic historiography of the Septuagint. Luke is undeniably interested in the Hebrew scriptural tradition, incorporating a significant quantity of echoes and allusions in his two volumes, demonstrating the Christological fulfillment of Old Testament truths. Moreover, Luke's specific regard for Deuteronomic history is well established with clear intertextuality to the Elijah and Elisha narrative, as prime examples.

Luke's Regard for Deuteronomy

Luke maintains a significant connection to Deuteronomy. This is compellingly argued by C. F. Evans. In his 1957 "Deuteronomy Hypothesis," he describes how the structure of Luke's central and core section—the travel narrative in Jerusalem, the lengthiest portion of his Gospel, much of which is unique content—is designed in parallel to portions of Deuteronomy. This "Deuteronomy Hypothesis" caught the attention of Lukan scholars, albeit with mixed reception. Joseph Fitzmyer and Craig Evans are examples of scholars who incorporate this theory into their works. Even those who are reluctant to affirm its arguments entirely still readily accept a significant portion of its Deuteronomic connections to the Lukan Gospel.

---

1. This chapter was first presented as a paper read at the Southeastern Regional Meeting of the Evangelical Theological Society held at Toccoa Falls College in Georgia on February 23, 2024.

CHAPTER 8: DEUTERONOMIC HISTORY AND THE PORTRAYAL OF SOLOMON

What prompts an interest in Luke's connection to Deuteronomy? One facet is the Mosaic emphasis in the Lukan corpus. For example, Acts 3 draws on Deut 18:15, applying the prophet-like Moses christologically. Additionally, scholars largely affirm that the new exodus motif is a Lukan priority.

Lukan Ethics of Greed

Luke is also interested in matters of greed and generosity, connected to his ethics regarding wealth and material possessions, another superbly attested Lukan paradigm. Mary's Magnificat, Luke 1:53, states the hungry are taken care of, while the wealthy are excluded. Luke's unique material concerning John the Baptist's response to various inquirers includes the ethics of greed and generosity, the sharing of cloaks and food, and the rebuttal of economic exploitation expected of tax collectors and soldiers (Luke 3:10–14). Remarkably, Jesus's Sermon on the Plain in Luke 6 juxtaposes the economically poor to the wealthy and the hungry to the well fed, and incorporates ethics of generous lending practices, which resorts to gifting. Other Lukan unique material includes the parable of the debtors (Luke 7), the good Samaritan (Luke 10), the rich fool (Luke 11), the trilogy of banquet statements in Luke 14, the prodigal son of Luke 15, the rich man and Lazarus (Luke 16), all prime examples of greed and generosity ethics.

Deuteronomic Motives for Lukan Literary Expressions

Having introduced two foundational aspects to Luke-Acts, the connections to Deuteronomy and greed, this study now considers potential motives for Lukan literary expressions. Luke is highly interested in political and economic exploitation, beyond the scope of this presentation; however, Deuteronomy itself warns of political greed.

To clarify, the focus of this chapter is to investigate theological significance. The hypothetical redactions or later tradition of Deuteronomy itself in relation to the historical genre and documentary hypothesis (JEDP) are intriguing but secondary.

Deuteronomic Ethical Principles for Kings as Applied to Solomon

Deuteronomy provides a fascinating code for Israel's kings. Wherein there are multiple eligibility factors for royalty, there are three core ethical principles that a king must maintain, essential to this study.

Principle One—Wives

Deuteronomy 17:17 instructs the king not to accumulate an excessive quantity of wives. No explicit barometer is provided to determine the appropriate quantitative boundaries; however, Solomon's seven hundred wives and three hundred concubines undoubtedly surpass that limit, not to mention his activities that may be unrecorded. This excess is clear evidence of greedy passions with Solomon's occupation with building his harem far beyond the scope of healthy behavior.

Solomon's matrimonial commitments weaken his resolve and divert his attention, realized by compromising the concerns of Deut 17:17, that the king's heart will be distracted, and Deut 17:15, that the king may not be a foreigner, yet when he is influenced by foreign wives, the effect is near equally negative, as the predominate pattern of idolatry in First and Second Kings begins with Solomon's tolerance of these practices, a decision apparently overriding his supernatural gift of wisdom.

Principle Two—Silver and Gold

Deuteronomy 17:17 also prohibits the king from accumulating high volumes of silver and gold. Again, the stipulation is vague, not specifying or distinguishing the appropriate from disproportionate. However, with the Solomon narratives of 1 Kings, silver and gold are mentioned in more frequency than anywhere else in the canonical corpus.

Solomon amasses significant wealth via multiple methods, including the solicitation of tribute from surrounding kings. First Kings 10:21 indicates the devaluation of silver, hinting that Solomon may have altered the supply mechanics of the market. In other words, as 1 Kgs 10 conveys, he could have acquired so much that the enormous supply drove prices down.

CHAPTER 8: DEUTERONOMIC HISTORY AND THE PORTRAYAL OF SOLOMON

Principle Three—Horses and Egypt

Deuteronomy 17:16 prohibits the king from accumulating excess horses, and as a sub provision, the king must certainly not return to Egypt for horses. The principal concern is that relational aspects to Egypt including economic partnership signals backwardation. Again, the acceptable quantity of horses is unclarified, but Solomon is attested to have twelve thousand horses in 1 Kings, likely demonstrating excess. Moreover, outside the Pentateuch, 1 Kings mentions Egypt more than any other canonical text excluding Isaiah and Jeremiah.

Solomon initiates a bitter process, beginning with a trade agreement with Egypt, receiving Pharaoh's daughter as wife. He ultimately secures horses from Egypt and enjoys favors from Pharaoh's army, raising the question of how his commercial alliance with Egypt may have contributed toward the temple's construction. Not long after his death, Egypt exploits Israel via the gateway introduced by Solomon.

Implications of the Violation of Deuteronomic Principles

Kings should not live above the people

The purpose of the royal mandates, noted in Deut 17:20, is to prevent the king from living above the people, something else Solomon violates. God dwells in Solomon's Temple, contrasting with the tabernacle construction. The narrative of 1 Kings is focused on Solomon's inspirational design, which is opposed to the divine structure in Exodus wherein God commands and Moses carries out God's commands. The seven-year temple construction with the enormously elaborate descriptive wealthy qualities is exceeded by the palace he builds for himself, a project amassing a time span of thirteen years, indicating his excessiveness and exuberance. The number thirteen is noteworthy. If the time frame had been fourteen years, it would have indicated seven times two, which would indicate twice as much of a something good, with the number seven symbolizing fullness, completeness. However, the number seven plus six indicates something suspect about the project. Could the palace's construction process take have taken nearly twice as long because Solomon required it to exhibit twice the quality of the temple of God?[2]

2. Curiously, 1 Kgs 10:14 notes the infamous "666" in relation to Solomon's gold, the

Kings should not rely on Egypt

As noted, a primary concern with the king's restrictions is enabling backward momentum to Egypt, while also avoiding an elevated monarch. Strikingly, Solomon's economy resembled that of Pharaoh's in Exodus, the antecedent of his father-in-law, with tremendous building projects, a strict work regiment, the exertion of political influence including internal and external exploitation through slavery and greediness toward the king of Hiram. Solomon even constructs handsome ships to secure more gold, albeit they never sail, an ongoing picture of excess.

Kings should represent all the people

Solomon's economic policies favored his home, the southern territory of Judah. As Jerusalem was elevated, so was its earning power. The northern majority of Israel plainly grew disenfranchised with his policy, evidenced by the ten tribes self-annexing after Solomon's demise, when his son Rehoboam served as a policy maker in the image and likeness of his father. Moreover, the idolatry indirectly introduced and assuredly tolerated by Solomon through his wives ignited a downward spiral in both the north and the south. This was even more true in the north, likely as a revolt against the Jerusalem temple cult that reflected the continuous imagery of Solomon's wealth.

Outcome of Solomon's Violations

Solomon's mistakes jeopardize the Davidic dynasty. God even initially blesses a covenant with Jeroboam, the opponent of a unified kingdom. Jeroboam's background is worth noting. His origins are from the slave-class, skilled-laborer sect, as an orphan and the son of a widow, making him an ideal representative from marginalized and vulnerable groups.

Another loose but striking connection occurs through the prophetic oracle of Jeremiah, another Lukan favorite. The prophet's temple sermon in Jer 7 includes a rebuke for submission to foreign gods, a Solomon-induced problem. Jeremiah also condemns the neglect of the orphans and widows. The books of First and Second Samuel, along with First and Second Kings, offer multiple attestations regarding orphans and widows, but

only place outside Revelation this number is utilized in canonical texts.

CHAPTER 8: DEUTERONOMIC HISTORY AND THE PORTRAYAL OF SOLOMON

none in relation to Solomon except for the reference to Jeroboam having been an orphan. Moreover, Jeremiah remarks on the ethical treatment of resident foreigners, while Solomon's forced slave labor in 1 Kgs 9 of resident aliens might qualify as a precursor to Jeremiah's concerns. Again, Jeroboam is the "anti-Solomon"; and while he is not a foreigner, he is a slave laborer, orphaned, and the son of a widow. Given Luke's favoritism toward the northern kingdom, which includes a Galilean and perhaps even a Samaritan bias, this interrelatedness merits note.

Solomon is provided opportunities that God offers to no other. On the heels of Saul's failures came David; yet, following David's events with Bathsheba and Uriah, the remainder of 2 Samuel casts many suspicious narratives of David's leadership, to say the least. However, with Solomon's rise, not only did the foreign and domestic policies begin in immaculate fashion, but he is also victorious over his enemies, and there are indications of spiritual vibrancy in the land. He communes with God in ways unique among Israel's kings. He impresses God with a request for wisdom, which he is granted in unprecedented volumes. Solomon provides some of the most qualitative speeches and prayers to be found in the Old Testament, certainly outperforming his royal counterparts both former and latter. The early portion of 1 Kings supplies the most optimistic, hopeful, and promising articulation of Israel's monarchical status. Despite this potential, however, Solomon's failures are Israel's undoing. Once the kingdom splits, the spiral accelerates.

References to Solomon in Luke-Acts

Having considered Luke's interest in wealth, possessions, greed, and Deuteronomy, in addition to the parallels between Deut 17 and 1 Kings, this study now addresses the five locations where Solomon is referenced in Luke-Acts. Luke's authorship tallies half the mentions of Solomon's name in the New Testament, with two of the traditions shared by the Matthean account, with some caveats. Additionally, the Hebrew prophetic traditions in the Old Testament only mention Solomon once, while the historic books Ezra and Nehemiah make only seven references, five being genealogical. Outside of First and Second Samuel, First and Second Kings, and the writings of the Chronicler, Solomon is sparsely regarded, especially compared with his father, David. Meanwhile, Luke uniquely evokes and incorporates Solomon into his narratives.

Luke 11:29–32

The first reference is Luke 11:29–32, shared in the Matthean tradition, when Jesus alludes to the sign of Jonah in verses 29 and 30, and again in 32. These create a literary bookend; sandwiched in the middle is the reference to Solomon in verse 31 declaring the Queen of the South will rise at the judgment with Jesus's contemporaries because she traveled to observe Solomon's wisdom but someone greater than Solomon is present. Solomon's witness was God's gift of wisdom, not preaching or appropriate ethics, which solicited the queen's response. Moreover, that events were not the ideal of Solomon's wisdom in application, the queen came frankly to view his wealth, as his material assets receive the most prominent and vivid description in 1 Kgs 10.

To determine how Solomon functions in this illustration is to know Jonah, who bookends his reference. Jonah was the least of Israel's canonical prophets, whereas his counterparts had reservations or hesitations, yet Jonah was beyond reluctant, he was thoroughly resistant, running away from his assignment. Throughout the book that bears his name, Jonah is the antithetical model of God's prophet. Some examples include his suspicious silence on the boat during the storm in Jonah 1 along with suicidal tendencies, his selfishness in prayer and rescue in Jonah 2, which amounts to a victim mentality, his partial proclamation to Nineveh in Jonah 3 where he omits the crucial opportunity of repentance from his prophecy; then in Jonah 4 he is resentful of the effective Ninevite repentance.

The point made by Jesus is that the worst prophet had the most profound results, in Nineveh of all places, producing the ideal description of repentance, right down to the livestock. Israel, the sacred people, had the best prophets, yet they did not repent. However, if Nineveh, the wicked place, responded to the dysfunctional prophet, how much more so should Galileans and Judeans respond to Jesus, the greatest prophet. Likewise, if the queen of Sheba inquires of Solomon given his imperfect, incomplete, and even corrupt witness, how much more should they adhere to Jesus. This Lukan pericope coincides with Deut 10:16–17 according to Evans's Deuteronomy Hypothesis, which among other things rebukes bribery while advocating justice for orphans, widows, and resident foreigners in context of material goods, while also throwing shade at Egypt.

CHAPTER 8: DEUTERONOMIC HISTORY AND THE PORTRAYAL OF SOLOMON

Luke 12:27

The author's second reference to Solomon, also in Luke's travel narrative, occurs in chapter 12: "Consider how the wildflowers grow. They do not labor or spin. Yet I tell you, not even Solomon in all his splendor was dressed like one of these" (12:27). Luke locates this quote in a different order than its counterpart reference in Matthew, reorganizing it to occur just before Jesus says, "Sell your possessions and give to the poor. Provide purses for yourselves that will not wear out, a treasure in heaven that will never fail, where no thief comes near and no moth destroys. For where your treasure is, there your heart will be also" (Luke 12:33–34). Having invoked Solomon's memory just prior to this statement, Luke presents Jesus's ethics as the antithetical representation of Israel's third king.

Moreover, immediately prior to this remarking regarding Solomon, Jesus tells the parable of Luke 12:13–21 about the sometimes-called "rich fool." The parable is prefaced by Jesus's admonition, "Watch out . . . and beware of all greed! Your life doesn't consist of the sum total of your possessions" (12:15). The wealthy fool indulges in excess to the extent that he instigates construction projects to secure greater storage, actions that are reminiscent of Solomon's. This evokes parallels from Deut 12:17–32, which warns against selfishness and idolatry regarding harvests.

Acts 3:11

The book of Acts includes three references to Solomon, the first in Acts 3:11: "While the man held on to Peter and John, all the people were astonished and came running to them in the place called Solomon's Portico." Luke makes note of the name of Solomon while referencing a location on the temple premises. Although it presents a tenuous connection, just prior to this, in verse 6, Peter states, "silver and gold, I do not have." This recalls the Deut 17 provision against excess gold and silver, which links to the reference to Solomon who is depicted in the Old Testament as having broken that prohibition. In contrast, as Luke develops his new temple theology, he is careful to point out that the principal apostles in Jerusalem attest to having no silver or gold.

Acts 5:12

The second mention of Solomon is Acts 5:12, which again makes note of Solomon's Portico. This reference comes immediately on the heels of the Ananias and Sapphire pericope, which accumulates verses 1 through 11. Their greed is obvious, with an echo to Achan's sin during the conquest of Josh 7, and there is also an allusion to Uzza in 2 Samuel and his imposition upon the ark of God, the priests Nadab and Abihu in Lev 10, as well as Hophni and Phineas, priests in 1 Samuel, all mentioned by commentators. Another loose connection, granted, but Solomon's name appears congruent with internal greed.

Acts 7:47

The concluding mention of Solomon in the Lukan corpus takes place in Stephen's speech of Acts 7, a narrative which continues to reinforce Luke's new temple theology. In the lengthiest speech of Acts, Stephen navigates Israel's history, including the transitory nature of the patriarchs and early tabernacle before negatively attesting in verse 47 "But it was Solomon who built a house for him." Luke, having a northern and diasporic bias, accused Solomon of making God stationary with the temple, when the movement of God is designed to be mobile, evoking Isaiah's question "how in the world can you build a house for God?"

Import of Luke's References to Solomon

Several strains of thought have been brought to bear to determine Luke's view of Solomon. First, Luke-Acts has an overwhelming interest in proclaiming economic ethics that decry greed. Second, the Lukan author shows an affinity with Deuteronomy, a book including provisions against wealthy kings. Third, Solomon violates multiple Deuteronomic precepts required of kings as evidenced in the narrative in 1 Kings. Finally, Luke references Solomon a disproportionately large number of times, more than any other New Testament author. Based on these observations, it is arguable that Luke intentionally presents Solomon negatively or greedily.

In each mention of Solomon in Luke-Acts, the allusions to Solomon cast suspicion—by including Solomon in the midst of references to Jonah, associating him with Israel's dysfunctional prophet, in Luke 11;

CHAPTER 8: DEUTERONOMIC HISTORY AND THE PORTRAYAL OF SOLOMON

by using Solomon's name between the contrast of the wealthy stockpiling food and the exhortation to relinquish wealth and not worry over tangible goods in Luke 12; by mentioning Solomon when Peter attests to having no silver or gold in Acts 3; by using Solomon's name in connection with the ecclesial response to Ananias and Sapphira's greedy behavior in Acts 5; and, finally, by identifying the unideal nature of Solomon's Temple via Stephen's comments in Acts 7. Although each occurs in a subtle way, each reference to Solomon in Luke-Acts supports the hypothesis that Luke's remarks point to a negative view of Solomon. While it takes work to connect these dots, multiple connections point to the idea that Luke's literary design intentionally invoked Solomon, who was ruled by greed rather than Deuteronomic principles for kings, as a foil to emphasize how Jesus's kingdom would not be ruled by greed.[3]

---

3. This selection offers further research opportunities to expand this material; likely the clearest is in terms of Luke's new temple theology, wherein Solomon was the imperfect and perhaps even builder of the First Temple, so the antithetic posture of Lukan Christianity is foundational for the eschatological replacement.

Chapter 9: Ears and Heart Circumcision in Luke-Acts

Introduction

IN ACTS 7, STEPHEN responds to his accusers by appealing to Israel's story as his defense. God's new work, as noted within the Lukan corpus, was a fulfillment of Jewish history, yet it involved some distinctions, including that the temple in Jerusalem, while having served its function, should not be seen as the exclusive housing place of God. The result of such assertions is that concepts of sacred space within first-century Judaism are disrupted by the conceptions of the early church in Acts.

Stephen, anticipating the rejection of his listeners to these ideas, likens them to their stubborn forefathers, accusing them of being uncircumcised, a heavy condemnation for ancient Jews; however, his premise is that they are uncircumcised in their hearts and ears (Acts 7:51). The Old Testament includes a connection between the heart and circumcision, but Stephen's coupling of circumcision with not only the heart but also the ears is unique and therefore worthy of examination. The fact that this portion is the lengthiest speech recorded in the book of Acts is indicative of its importance as a crucial theological narrative. To uncover the meaning behind this connection, this study investigates the concept of ear and heart circumcision in Luke-Acts by first considering Old Testament attestations of circumcision, hearts, and ears, comparing those findings with a survey of the same three concepts in the Lukan corpus, and finally synthesizing the findings to discover the meaning behind Stephen's description of ears and heart circumcision.

CHAPTER 9: EARS AND HEART CIRCUMCISION IN LUKE-ACTS

Circumcision in the Old Testament

The initial instance of circumcision in the Hebrew scriptures is found in Gen 17:10–27, when God expresses to Abraham a condition to the covenant whereby all males must be circumcised on their eighth day. This stipulation applied not only to those born of the Abrahamic lineage, but also included all males within the household, even foreigners and slaves. Abraham's compliance is demonstrated when both Ishmael and Isaac are circumcised (Gen 21:4). The next reference to this practice and the final one in Genesis (34:14–24) occurs when the potential marital suitor for Dinah, daughter of Jacob, is required to enter the covenant through circumcision. Unquestionably, circumcision is viewed as a distinct covenant marker in Genesis.

Circumcision reappears in the Mosaic context beginning with Exod 4:26, when it is imperative for Moses to receive the mark to initiate his sacred vocation. Then, when Exod 12:43–49 gives the provision and the commandments for the Passover observance, the text records circumcision as a requirement extending even to foreigners who partake in the event. Finally, in Lev 12:1–3, guidance is given to postpartum women, reiterating the requirement of male circumcision on the eighth day. Then, Deut 10:16 proposes the circumcision of the heart, which will be further developed in a subsequent section. Later, as the Israelites prepare for the conquest of Canaan, Joshua (5:2–8) mandates that all males entering the promised land must be circumcised.

The prophet Jeremiah (9:25–26) extends the ideas of circumcision. In this context, God laments that he must judge the covenant people. However, at the narrative's conclusion, a new concept is introduced, contrasting the circumcision of the flesh with that of the heart as first referenced in Deut 10:16. The idea Jeremiah expresses is that those who receive the mark on their hearts are true bearers of the seal, while those who carry the mark on their flesh alone are worthy of judgment.

The Hebrew scriptures also make several references to uncircumcision. In Judg 14, Samson's parents are disappointed in his decision to wed a bride from the uncircumcised peoples, indicating the importance of this ritual as an ethnic marker. Also in Judg 15:18, Samson laments the possibility of falling into, and dying by, the hands of the uncircumcised Philistines. In 1 and 2 Samuel and 1 Chronicles, the enemies of Israel, particularly the Philistines, are referred to as the "uncircumcised" with disdain (1 Sam 14:6,

17:26, 17:36, 31:4; 2 Sam 1:20; 1 Chr 10:4), continuing the expression of circumcision as an ethnic distinction.

The prophetic writings draw on deeper theological concepts regarding uncircumcision. Isaiah 52:1 contrasts and compares the beautiful clothes of restored Jerusalem to the uncircumcised and unclean nations that had taken them into captivity. Habakkuk 2:16 records that the prophet stands watch, and an oracle against Babylon is given remarking that, in judgment, the empire will be shamed and their uncircumcision exposed (2:16). Ezekiel deals extensively with the concept of uncircumcision, specifically in his remarks concerning judgment. He uses the designation in a derogatory manner in reference to the gentiles (Ezek 28:10; 31:18; 32:19, 21, 24–26, 28–30, 32). However, in Ezek 44, the prophet employs language that is sparse among his canonical counterparts: particularly, in reference to gentiles, he uses the phrase "uncircumcised in heart and flesh" (Ezek 44:7, 9).

Jeremiah, in the context of temple worship, remarks on those uncircumcised in "heart and flesh" as desecrating the sacred location. Likewise, Jeremiah (9:25–27) writes concerning oracles of judgment, whereby he mentions those judged by God include not only the nations who are uncircumcised, but also Israel, which is uncircumcised in heart.

Both Jeremiah and Ezekiel likely utilize Lev 26:41 and Deut 10:16 as a premise for the concept of heart circumcision. Although the prophetic writings also support the concept of circumcision as a distinguishing sociocultural, ethnic, and religious marker as depicted within the Pentateuch and historical writings, they also develop the concept further by comparing fellow Israelites to the uncircumcised and by denoting a supportive circumcision of the heart as reflecting inward qualities.

A synthesis of the Old Testament findings is that circumcision was a practice with the function of ethnic distinction as well as religious devotion. In the post-exilic age, the practice became more intentionally and consciously an ethnic identity marker as the socio-cultural boundaries were increasingly threatened, and during that time, the practice also later became associated more heavily with morality among some in first-century Judaism.[1]

---

1. Niehoff, "Circumcision," 89–123.

CHAPTER 9: EARS AND HEART CIRCUMCISION IN LUKE-ACTS

Ears in the Old Testament

Because the usage of the word *ears* is so prolific in the Hebrew scriptures, the preliminary stage of investigation categorizes two crucial elements—liturgical and practical. First, while the liturgical component may involve secondary, seemingly subtle, material, these observations offer a vibrant element that will help to develop circumcision in Luke-Acts.

The liturgical component is first found in Gen 35:4, when God instructs Jacob to return to Bethel to build an altar. Before he sets out on his journey, Jacob commands his group to purify themselves and to get rid of foreign gods. One significant element in describing this process is that the people gave Jacob the rings worn in the ear. This makes it clear that part of the consecration for Jacob to return to "the house of the Lord" was connected to the ear. Secondly, in Exod 29:20 and Lev 8:23-24, a rite for the priesthood is recorded whereby Aaron and his sons are to have the blood of a ram placed on their earlobes. Here, the ear symbolizes, to some extent, the ordination of the priesthood. Meanwhile, Lev 14:14–28 records a purification ritual conducted by the priests for a ceremonial cleansing, whereby blood is placed on the ear. In another critical section, the practice of ear piercing is an identity marker applied by Hebrews to their slaves (Exod 21:6). Then, when Aaron leads the people to build a golden calf, his specific instructions are to bring the gold rings that were worn on the ears, an instance in which corruption is associated with the jewelry of the ear (Exod 32:2–3). While one should be careful not to overstate this, this survey establishes a concept in the Hebrew narratives regarding ears as connected to consecration, ceremonial purity, and idolatry.

The second critical aspect is found in a more practical approach—simply, the act of hearing that takes place in the relationship between God and humanity. Isaiah and Jeremiah are excellent sources demonstrating the practical regard for ears within the Hebrew canon. Simply put, they are concerned at times with whether God will close his ears or remain attentive to the cries of the people (Isa 59:1). More prominently, they question whether the people will incline their ears to God or be dismissive of his messengers (Isa 55:3, Jer 13:15). In other instances, it appears that God closes the ears of the people following their persistent rejection and rebellion (Isa 6:10, Jer 5:21). The ear as a spiritual metaphor represents a deep theological resource that appears extensively in Old Testament writings to indicate the receptiveness of the covenant people to the oracles and mandates of God.

Hearts in the Old Testament

The human heart is another ubiquitous word found throughout the corpus of the Hebrew canonical writings. A brief synopsis of the heart in the Old Testament determines that, first, the Pentateuch and Joshua affirm that the heart is the core human self (Gen 6:5, Lev 19:17, Exod 7:23, Deut 11:18), the source of human motivations (Gen 20:6, Exod 4:24, Deut 6:5–6), including repentance (Exod 8:13–14, 35:21; Deut 4:29; Josh 24:23), from which comes sin (Gen 6:5, Num 15:39, Deut 29:18–19). The historical books convey that God searches the hearts of people (1 Chr 29:17) who might turn to him wholeheartedly (1 Sam 7:3; 1 Kgs 9:4, 11:3–9; 2 Chr 15:12).

The prophets again contribute meaningfully, employing the term *heart* extensively to represent the inner self (Isa 49:21, Jer 13:22, Ezek 14:3), a place of false security and sin (Isa 47:10, Jer 5:23–24, Ezek 3:7), a guardian of true teaching (Isa 51:7), and as associated with purification or defilement (Jer 4:14) and repentance (Jer 24:7). The minor prophets also affirm the heart as the core inner self (Hos 7:6), the agent of repentance (Joel 2:12–13, Zech 10:7, Hos 13:6), and the source of pride, false confidence, and sin (Obad 1:3; Zeph 1:12; Zech 7:10, 8:17).

The final element to consider in this brief Old Testament survey of the heart consists of unique features primarily contained within the major prophets. Jeremiah includes a promise of restoration, describing that "they shall be my people, and I will be their God" (NRSV Jer 32:38), and the text then further elaborates what this will look like—that it will involve heart transformation, becoming an everlasting covenant (32:39–40). Furthermore, Ezek 11 articulates the removal of evil and the placement of a new heart and spirit within the people, so that God's commandments will be kept (11:19–20). The goal of this action echoes Jeremiah when Ezekiel writes, "Then they shall be my people, and I will be their God" (11:20). Ezekiel then reiterates this idea (36:25–28) when writing about the reconciliation, attesting that God will clean his people and grant a new heart and spirit to enable them to be law-keepers. These same two prophets are the ones who significantly articulated heart circumcision in Ezek 44:7–9 and Jer 9:26, discussed in previous sections.[2]

The concepts of *heart* in the Hebrew texts contain depth but are straightforward in their meaning. The heart is the inner core of the human

---

2. An additional text of interest comes from Exod 28 when instructions are given concerning the priestly vestments. The priest is to wear the breastplate of judgment, because he is bearing the judgment for all Israel on his heart (28:29–30).

CHAPTER 9: EARS AND HEART CIRCUMCISION IN LUKE-ACTS

self from which all motivations flow. When sin and rebellion exist, they come from the heart. When the prophets decree repentance, this also must be complied with from the heart.

Ears in Luke-Acts

For Luke, the ears serve as a preceptor and filter of gospel truth. Because Luke is unique in connecting the ears with the heart and circumcision, a study of the ears in the overarching Luke-Acts text is considered next in discovering the author's meaning. This section will highlight each usage of *ous* ("ears") in Luke-Acts.[3]

Luke's first use of the word *ous* in the Gospel occurs in the infancy narrative. It comes after the annunciation to Mary and her journey to visit Elizabeth, who is carrying John the Baptist, the other miracle child (Luke 1:30–45). Elizabeth's ears are referenced as hearing Mary's greeting, which prompts the child in her womb to leap because Elizabeth is filled with the Holy Spirit (1:44). In Luke-Acts, Elizabeth becomes the first person to respond to Jesus while he is still carried in Mary's womb, and the response is one of joy, a deep and profound theological term for Luke.

Luke's second and third uses of *ous* occur in Jesus's early ministry. The second use of *ous* is in conjunction with the important occasion in Luke 4:21 when Jesus returns to Nazareth and gives a reading of Isaiah in the synagogue on a Sabbath. Jesus concludes affirming that the reading has been fulfilled in the ears of his audience. At that point, the narrative turns to the crowd's response, which unlike Elizabeth's, is not one of joy, but of rejection. The third instance is in Luke 8:8 when Jesus delivers the parable of the sower, concluding with the remark, "Those with ears, let them hear." Again, this is indicative of the reception of theological truth.

The final examples of *ous* in Luke occur within the travel narrative to Jerusalem. The fourth occasion takes place in Luke 9:44 at the commencement of the travel narrative. Jesus prepares his disciples by informing them of rich gospel material, namely his fate in Jerusalem, and prefaces this truth by admonishing them, "place these words into your [*ous*]" as critical information is transmitted. The fifth example of *ous* in Luke-Acts comes in Luke

---

3. The use of *ous* that has been excluded in this chapter is the instance in Luke 22:50–51, when Peter cuts off the ear of the priest's servant. This involves a different context in the use of the ears, potentially lending itself to an allegorical treatment, but that is outside the scope of this study.

14:35, which again follows the formula of declaring "those with ears, let them hear," as a response to truth shared via the nature of discipleship.

Three more examples of *ous* occur in the book of Acts. In the sixth example in the Lukan corpus, Acts 7:51, Stephen remarks how his words, as well as the testimonies from Scripture, have been rejected; and he declares that his listeners, who are preparing to stone him, are uncircumcised in heart and *ous*. The attackers' ears are evidently unconsecrated and unreceptive. Significantly, the physical actions of Stephen's audience are indicative of their covenant blame, as they cover their ears to avoid hearing Stephen's words (Acts 7:57).

The seventh example is again paired with an expression of deep theological truth. Peter had just given a defense of his actions in the home of Cornelius, a position which in turn becomes a significant milestone in Acts. After this occasion, upon the call of Barnabas and Saul of Tarsus, the narrative focus shifts from Jerusalem to the Antioch church. Acts 11:22 records that the report of the Antioch church was "heard in the *ous*" of the Jerusalem church.

The final instance of *ous* in Luke-Acts takes place in Acts 28:27. Here, Paul quotes Isa 6:10 concerning God closing the ears of the people. This was referenced by Paul upon the assessment that some of his Jewish audience in Rome received his words, while others rejected them.

All these instances confirm that when Luke employs the word *ous*, the context is that of receiving and perceiving the truth of the gospel.

Hearts in the Gospel of Luke

There are twenty references to *kardia* ("heart") in Luke and another nineteen in Acts. The first three in Luke occur early in the Gospel, twice in reference to John the Baptizer. He will "turn the hearts of the fathers toward their children," and those who heard the unusual circumstances of John's birth "kept them in their hearts" and speculated on the potential greatness of the child (Luke 1:17, 1:66) Meanwhile, in her hymn of praise, Mary expresses God's victory over those with pride in their hearts (1:51). Three more occasions are associated with Jesus's birth. First, Mary reflects in her heart on the experiences in Bethlehem (2:19) and the later happenings with Jesus at the temple (2:51); then, oracles proclaim that Jesus will reveal the hearts of many (2:35). At this point, for the author of Luke, use of the word *heart* represents a place of reflection and disposition.

CHAPTER 9: EARS AND HEART CIRCUMCISION IN LUKE-ACTS

Next, in Luke 3:15, the crowds were questioning in their hearts if John could be the Messiah, followed by Jesus speaking to those who are questioning and doubting in their hearts (Luke 5:22). Jesus teaches concerning the heart, relating it to the core of the person from which come good and evil, as well the place from which speech is derived (Luke 6:45). However, in the parable of the sower, Jesus affirms that those with good characteristics of the heart can receive the kingdom (Luke 8:15), juxtaposed with those whose hearts the devil can prevent God's word from reaching (Luke 8:12). The heart continues to be affirmed as a conduit of thinking in Luke 9:47, Luke 12:45, and Luke 21:14 and is connected to love and commandment-keeping in Luke 10:27. Finally, since God knows the hearts of men who attempt to justify themselves (Luke 16:15), it appears that the heart is the deeper core of human substance, affirming that the heart is connected to personal values (Luke 12:34).

The first two of three post-resurrection mentions of the heart are made by Jesus when the heart is labeled as the source of belief and doubt (Luke 24:25, 24:38). Finally, in Luke 24:32, the Emmaus disciples feel a burning in their hearts in response to their encounter with Jesus. Consistent with the Old Testament material, the Gospel affirms that this organ metaphorically functions as the core of the human self, and as the basis for inner motivations, reflection, and decision making. However, it also factors into a person's response to theological truth.

Hearts in the Acts of the Apostles

The nineteen instances of *heart* in the book of Acts concur with the findings from Luke's Gospel. The author's use of *kardia* in Acts affirms that God knows the heart, or true identity, of each person (1:24, 8:21, 13:22, 15:9, 21:13). The heart remains the source of motivation (5:4, 8:21, 11:23), is a respondent to truth (2:26, 15:8–9, 16:14, 28:27), including conviction (2:37), and is depicted as being contrary to God (7:39, 7:51, 8:21–22, 28:27). It is also presumed that members of the new covenant community could be influenced in their hearts by Satan (5:3). Furthermore, in Acts, the concept of church unity relates to the heart. First, in 2:46 a description of fellowship mentions the motivations of the heart. Then in 4:32, the group was of a single heart, and this propelled them to live as a household and share all their goods.

Perhaps the most significant event involving the heart in Acts is tied to the work of the Holy Spirit among the gentiles that prompted the Jerusalem Council to convene at the midpoint of Acts. Therein, it is confirmed that the Holy Spirit's work was not distinct between Jew and gentile, as the latter also received a pure heart (15:9), a fulfillment of Old Testament prophetic indications. This is a critical statement related to the proposed ethnic unity of the early church.

Circumcision in Luke-Acts

Luke employs the word "circumcision" sparingly in his two-volume work; however, when engaging with the topic, he does so strategically. The Gospel only mentions the rite twice, when John the Baptist and Jesus are circumcised (1:59, 2:21). Since both characters' biographic material is important to Luke's introduction, the rite is affirmed; however, for both children, the event also provides the opportunity for broader prophetic oracles to ensue.

The book of Acts devotes more space to discussing the ritual. The first mention of circumcision is encountered in Stephen's speech (7:1–60), responding to accusations that he was refuting the customs of his ancestors, including the law. In his defense, Stephen recounts Hebrew history beginning with Abraham, who was given the covenant of circumcision which he passed on to Isaac (7:8). Stephen continues by recounting the exodus narrative, Israel's rebellions, and Solomon's Temple. Stephen's thesis is clarified when he quotes Isa 66:1 to articulate that God is not confined to any sacred space, using the mobility of Jewish history to reinforce this concept (7:48–50). He then charges his audience with the stubbornness of their ancestors who rejected God's servants, at which point he describes them as being uncircumcised in heart and ears (7:51–53). Upon hearing this, the crowd covers their ears while stoning Stephen (7:56–60).

The next remarks concerning circumcision are connected to the remarkable events in Acts 10 concerning Cornelius, who receives Peter in his home, hears the apostolic message, and experiences reception of the Holy Spirit. At the time of this event, this compels Peter's circumcised companions to reflect that even the uncircumcised gentiles received the same experience (10:45). Moreover, in the companion narrative, Peter returns to Jerusalem where the circumcised believers question the legitimacy of Peter's encounter with Cornelius (11:2), specifically that he was in the

CHAPTER 9: EARS AND HEART CIRCUMCISION IN LUKE-ACTS

company of the uncircumcised (11:3). However, they, too, are convinced of the validity of the experience upon hearing Peter's witness.

The event with Cornelius's household leads to momentum of the movement among the gentiles. Upon noting this trajectory, a council is called in Jerusalem in Acts 15, primarily for determining the movement's stance on matters of circumcision among these new believers (15:5). The determination is made that for these non-Jews, the ritual is unnecessary, since ample evidence exists of the work having been completed in their hearts (15:9). Immediately following the Jerusalem Council, the adjacent narrative records Timothy, whose mother is Jewish but whose father is Greek, embarking with Paul on his missionary journeys, whereupon he is circumcised, presumably, as half-Jewish, to comply with ethnic precedent and to avoid distractions in their synagogue ministry (16:3). The final remark on circumcision in Acts occurs in 21:21. Upon Paul's return to Jerusalem, he is accused of teaching that circumcision is unnecessary for both Jews and gentiles. Paul does not defend himself regarding that specific charge, nor does the narrative completely clarify this matter.

These instances of circumcision in Luke-Acts demonstrate that physical circumcision is applied to John the Baptist and Jesus in conjunction with prophetic oracles, and to Timothy in connection to his calling to accompany the Pauline mission. Other than those instances, it is remarked upon in terms of Israel's patriarchal history. In terms of theological development, the Jerusalem Council determines the practice to be unnecessary for the gentile believers, emphasizing that physical circumcision is a matter that should not disrupt fellowship between Jewish and gentile Christians. However, in the theology of Luke-Acts, drawn from the prophetic tradition of the Old Testament, the internal mark of circumcision is the imperative sign for both Jews and gentiles, particularly according to the reflections of Jeremiah (9:25–27, 32:38–40) and Ezekiel (11:19–20, 36:25–28, 44:7–9) asserted through Stephen's remarks to his fellow Jews (Acts 7:51–53), and also reinforced in statements regarding heart purity at the Jerusalem Council of gentiles (Acts 15:5–9).

Synthesis

In summary, Luke, who is very interested in Jewish scriptural tradition, tends to draw on a tapestry of Old Testament thought, particularly concentrated on Jeremiah and Ezekiel, in conveying his doctrine of circumcision. This expression of theology regarding heart circumcision fits Luke's agenda of a gospel transmission to the broader gentile world, extending beyond diasporic synagogue Jews "unto the ends of the earth" (Acts 1:8). As the overarching narrative of Luke-Acts heads toward Rome, the message Luke demonstrates is that the early church, while being of the lineage of Israel's story, offers non-Jews a distinct approach. Gentiles are not required to be initiated into socio-cultural ethnic Israel through the sign of the fleshly identity marker to become disciples of Jesus. Rather, what is important to Luke is that the ears of the people should be able to listen to the good news, and that their hearts, the seat of their dispositions, should be circumcised.

In the same way that circumcision of the flesh was a purity marker of Second Temple Judaism, so also, to Luke, the circumcision of ears and hearts become such a marker within the early church. Mary Douglas attests that Hebrew scriptures maintain an interest in human orifices as a surrogate for the social orifices, the entry and exit points of the collective.[4] Likewise, John Pilch notes that inconsistencies are a sign of impurity in Jewish thinking.[5]

This study in relation to circumcision in Luke-Acts invites further dialogue with Douglas, Pilch, and others, not only regarding circumcision as a purity marker in Second Temple Judaism associated with the male genital, a physical orifice, but also concerning how the Old Testament prophets, specifically Jeremiah and Ezekiel, proclaim Israel's inconsistency through maintaining the physical marker without the inward sign. In the context of Pilch's assertion, genital circumcision without heart circumcision renders a state of uncleanliness. Moreover, when Stephen accuses his audience of being uncircumcised in heart and ears, it can be inferred that he asserts that they are inconsistent. Therefore, according to Pilch's theory, Stephen's indictment would render them unclean, at least in the perspectives of Luke's ideal readers.

For Luke, the human orifice of the ear metaphorically replaces the male genitalia as the human orifice, indicating the social purity of the early church. This may perhaps be not only because the concept of ear and heart circumcision would be ethnically inclusive, a clear Lukan agenda, but also because it would be gender inclusive, another matter close to Luke's heart. These factors merit additional exploration.

---

4. Douglas, *Purity and Danger*, 144.
5. Pilch and Malina, *Handbook of Biblical Social Values*, 147–48.

Chapter 10: Father, Son, and Spirit

Symbols of Patronage and Reciprocity in Luke-Acts

Introduction

THE WORLD OF LUKE-ACTS was a collectivistic society; therefore, an operational awareness of such a cultural setting is vital toward grasping societal variables perceived by the Lukan author and audience. While collectivism incorporates some complex features, many of these conditions are generally understood. Group-oriented societies stand in contrast to the individualism of the contemporary United States and much of the Western world. In the ancient world no virtues such as "rugged individualism" (as those from the United States would understand the expression) existed.[1] Rather, in collectivistic cultures, identity is referred to as dyadic—embedded within, determined by, and inseparable from the community. To function with any societal regard, everyone was required to be networked. When it came to business arrangements, even in agrarian life, success was only made feasible through connectivity.

Luke incorporates the qualities of patron-client relationships, well known to him and his Mediterranean audience, to convey the theological functions of God, Jesus, the Holy Spirit, and of human participation and response.[2]

---

1. The parable of the prodigal son (Luke 15:11–32) as an example illustrates the complexities of collectivistic life when he essentially acts independently of the familial unit.

2. Originally presented on February 25, 2023, at Columbia International University (Columbia, South Carolina) for the Southeastern Region of the Evangelical Theological Society Annual Meeting.

Patronage in Collectivistic Society

Such a social environment produces the system of patronage, a relational entity necessary for moving both tangible and intangible goods. The patron-client system is the result of the disparity of social classes, whereby the small number of ruling elites control, govern, and influence virtually all matters of life. This is especially so in agrarian communities like the vast majority of first-century Palestine, which was largely made up of peasants, artisans, day laborers, and some slaves.

Patrons

In such relationships, the patron is the individual with resources, generally of a high honor status. Frequently these patrons controlled land, money, social positions, and commodities. Accordingly, they were positioned to select who might be granted access to which assets. For example, a patron would serve as a creditor, extending a monetary loan to debtors or supply land to tenant farmers.

Clients and Brokers

The client, at the reverse end of the patronage relationship, is the one who needs access to the goods controlled and provided by the patron. However, in some cases, a social elitist patron would have been largely unavailable to a potential client. For example, in a world where the vast majority of persons existed at or near subsistent levels, the wealthiest individuals either resided separately from the subsistent class or were surrounded by social layers that served as relational buffers.

In such cases, to establish relationships between patrons and clients, an intermediate party was required, called brokers. Simply put, these brokers would connect patrons and clients, serving as a mediator in negotiations as the primary or even the exclusive communication vessel. The broker in many cases was also responsible for the transfer of goods. Naturally, those positioned to advocate between the social classes benefited from a degree of moderately higher honor (and wealth) than the majority populace, although they would still retain a lower status than the patrons.

CHAPTER 10: FATHER, SON, AND SPIRIT

Patrons, Brokers, and Clients in the Parable of the Wicked Tenant

The parable of Luke 20:9–20 offers a simple application exemplifying this patron-client model. Sometimes called the parable of the wicked tenants, it includes a landowner who lives apart from this particular real estate holding, as many wealthy land patrons did, having accumulated significant portions of land. The patron would grant access to tenant farmers or clients, presumably agrarian peasants, a social group which included a large segment of those who had been displaced, having lost their ancestral land due to unfavorable economic policies and conditions that served to benefit the wealthy, land-owning elitists. At harvest, the patron would send his representatives, or brokers, to secure payment (likely in the form of produce). However, in the story, these resentful clients abuse the brokers. Eventually, the patron sends his son, remarking on the noticeable elevation of events, with clear expectations that the clients are aware of the son's greater standing. This parable has complex nuances as does the system of patronage, as with any relational dynamic. Still, this story does provide a helpful glimpse into the function of patronage and its import within the New Testament.

Patronage in Luke-Acts

Before making a more extensive application, it is suitable to acknowledge the body of existing scholarly works regarding patronage in the Lukan corpus. Other useful studies have applied the concept of patronage to specific isolated texts, largely parables. However, three specific sources offer a broader indication of how this patronage model is utilized in Luke-Acts, albeit within a limited framework. Eric Heen in his "Radical Patronage in Luke-Acts"[3] and Amanda Miller in her "Cut from the Same Cloth: A Study of Female Patrons in Luke–Acts and the Roman Empire,"[4] both articles, identify useful and appropriate reconfigurations of social constructs in Luke-Acts by applying the patronage model; however, their work does not engage with any trinitarian aspects. Meanwhile, Halvor Moxnes, in his chapter "Patron-Client Relations and the New Community of Luke-Acts,"[5] provides an adequate explanation of the roles of God, Jesus, and the apostles in terms of patronage, sonship, and brokerage; however, the Spirit's

---

3. Heen, "Radical Patronage," 445–58.
4. Miller, "Cut from Same Cloth," 203–10.
5. Moxnes, "Patron-Client Relations," 241–68.

participation is omitted. This study uniquely engages the Spirit more thoroughly within this paradigm, considering the potentials of this model not only in trinitarian and apostolic applications, but also in connection with the reciprocal obligations of the early church. This topic has many robust features, and the discussion is a conduit for further discovery.

God as Patron

Likely, the clearest and least contested representation is the assertion that God (the Father) is patron within this model. It is largely presumed that God (as a patron) is in the superior position of power, control, influence, and honor when dealing with both his covenant people as well as his broader creation. Moreover, God (as a patron) is the one who provides gifts that cannot be repaid in kind. Alternatively framed, God grants access to goods that are otherwise inaccessible. More specifically, as God bestows favor to his church, so also an obligation is required from the church. (Matters of reciprocity will be addressed later.) The programmatic initial proclamation by Jesus in Luke-Acts is the *euangelizō* of God's special year of favor and benefits (Luke 4:18–20). Simply put, this means that God, the patron, is open to doing business.

Fatherhood as Patronage

Within patriarchal societies, the head of household status is socially synonymous with fatherhood. Therefore, it is understandable how the characteristics of paternity are used as the imagery for patronage. The word *patron* is derived from *patēr* ("father"), providing not only a conceptual connection but also a linguistic link. Luke employs *father* as a description for God, which, in a unique, strategic way, denotes a special relationship. It is in part an indication of family, as the early church practiced in its kinship model. However, the basis of the church's kinship model was not being of the same blood; instead, it was being of the household of God. The Father, or patron, and his gift, the Spirit, served as a substitute for blood. To be clear, it is not necessary to dichotomize the structure in terms of either/or when it comes to considering kinship and patronage. Rather, a noticeable degree of overlaps between the categories are present, and one need not exclude the other. However, in antiquity, essentially and pragmatically, a patron would adopt clients into something that resembled a familial relationship. Fatherhood in

Luke-Acts is patronage, a factor not unique to the Lukan writings but also reflected in the household of God in Ephesians 2:19 and in the patronage of Caesar in Phil 4:22, where Paul speaks of Caesar's household, referring to the patronage aspects of those in the highest authority of government.

As Luke's further usage of father as a metaphor for God is considered, the more patronage is highlighted. Luke 10:21 conveys the father has revealed particular secrets to his select group of clients. In Luke 11:11–13, the father gives good gifts, appropriately understood as patronage language. This is reinforced in Luke 12:30 and 32 where the father takes care of clients' needs. This argument does not insist on subordinating the attributes of fatherhood to those of patronage; however, it does assert that these aspects frequently overlap both in the world of antiquity and in the modern world. Readers understand fatherhood to be a role as well as a biological representation. Sometimes, these two facets align, and sometimes they do not. At times, fatherhood is a component that functions entirely aside from DNA. This was not an alien concept to the ancient world. However, while adoption was relevant in antiquity, Luke-Acts does not utilize adoption language; instead Luke elects to portray patronage qualities.

Jesus as Son and Broker

Sonship offers another critical component in understanding patronage relationships. While a son might broker on behalf of his father, the son would enjoy a higher status than a broker. In this paradigm, Jesus functions as the son, higher than a broker, but also serving as a broker himself. One distinction is that the son functions in much more than a representative role for the father; he serves as a substitute for the father. Likewise, while on many occasions, a broker would have a unique self-interest, the son's interests are much more vested and shared with those of the father. Accordingly, the son stands to inherit the father's assets and has likely already been ascribed his father's honor. Therefore, the status of sonship is of great importance and of higher honor than that of an ordinary broker whose responsibilities could be given even to a responsible slave.

The Patron's Gift

Following Jesus's resurrection, *father* is employed in successive instances in Luke-Acts, each in relation to the Holy Spirit and the Pentecost event. In

Luke 24:49 and Acts 1:4, Jesus instructs his disciples to wait for the *epangelia* ("promise") of the Father. *Epangelia*, not unlike the English word *promise* or *guarantee*, can denote a variety of implications. While the English word *promise* maintains a core meaning, it functions distinctly based on context. Consider the following English examples—a promise to return home to one's family each night; a promise before one's bishop and God to uphold ordination vows; or a signature on a promissory note for legal purposes. Similarly, *epangelia* had a broad range of implications, including its use in legal contexts and economic transactions in a patronage context. In addition to the *epangelia ho patēr*, "promise of the Father," from Luke 24:49 and Acts 1:4, the description is applied in Acts 2:33. Meanwhile, *father* is also used in association with Spirit in Acts 1:7–8. This author's assertion is that this concept of the father's promise conveys the currency or commodity of trade within the patron-client dynamic in Luke-Acts.

The Holy Spirit—The Father's Promise

Having briefly argued for God as patron, the aspect of this study most accepted by scholars, attention turns next to the Holy Spirit. The Spirit's role with the patronage paradigm is to function as the promise, gift, or currency exchanged; it is the inaccessible commodity offered by the patron (God) to his clients. First, it should be noted that scholarship at times does injustice to the Jewishness of Luke-Acts. Much attestation has been offered as to the gentile qualities of the Lukan corpus and to its author. Meanwhile, some critical scholarship has sought to view Luke in terms of anti-Jewishness. However, Luke frequently brings uniquely Jewish features to the text. He may very well have been writing to gentiles, but he did so by telling an authentically Jewish story.

Salvation and Covenant

It would be a mistake to view the mind of the first-century Jewish follower of Jesus monolithically. Hebrew tradition already included some provisions for gentiles to convert to Jewish faith and practice and to participate in circumcision (Exod 12:48–49). In addition, Luke provides some of the most attested data regarding the "god fearing" sect of gentiles (Acts 10:2, 13:16). On the other hand, Jews would have considered that salvation and covenant had already been given to them. As Jesus and his apostles were attempting a movement in continuity with Judaism, so also, to Jewish Christians in the first century, salvation was continuous. The new covenant was not a break from traditional Hebrew faith, but a continuation of it. Therefore, collectively, the Israelites and their descendants were God's clients in the patronage relationship. The call of repentance in Acts was not a call to convert from Judaism to Christianity. Instead, it was a call (at least to the Jews) to reconsider Jesus.

Forgiveness and Exile

However, without attempting to limit the soteriological aspects of the Spirit, other worthwhile benefits are attached to the promise of the Father. One is the forgiveness of sins. This is admittedly and obviously soteriological; however, it merits distinct treatment. N. T. Wright correctly summarizes certain facets of first-century Judaism, largely their self-affirming view of being covenant-bearers, while simultaneously recognizing that sins had yet to be fully forgiven.[6] Consistent to this thinking is that forgiveness, in entirety, amounts not just to a cognitive or spiritual reality, but also to a full restoration of the people of God.

Naturally, with the persistence of foreign dominance that had largely been in effect since the sixth century BCE, contingent with the Roman occupation in the first-century context, all as the result of covenant disobedience, it would be conceivable for Jews to have believed that the exile was continuous. Other factors resembling exile included a large remaining dispersed populace, the massive loss of local indigenous land ownership, the exploitation of locally produced commodities, and the taxation being funneled to Jerusalem and Rome. The temple in Jerusalem was under the patronage of the Herodian dynasty and indirectly to Rome itself, with the high priest appointed by these rulers. Regarding this temple, Wright maintains that no imagery or clear affirmation of God's return exists.[7] The record of events regarding the dedication of the tabernacle and Solomon's Temple, namely the presence of God descending, are absent with regard to the Second Temple in both Old Testament and Second Temple Jewish texts. These factors led many Jews to believe that sins were not forgiven, that God had not returned to Zion, and that their exile was extended.

---

6. Wright, *Jesus and the Victory of God*, 354.
7. Wright, *New Testament and the People of God*, 269.

Limited Good Society

The forgiveness of sin, the temple, and full restoration are inseparable from the Holy Spirit. To fully grasp the significance of God (the patron's) gift of the Spirit, one must understand not only the historical elements present, but also other social considerations, including the implications of a limited good society. The basic definition of this cultural mechanism is that everything considered socially and/or personally desirable was viewed as being not only in great demand, but also in limited supply. Modern Western readers understand the principle of supply and demand in the context of contemporary capitalism. The rule of thumb, in all economies, is that as demand grows higher and supply dwindles, inflation takes effect. In a limited good society, a criterion that sociologists apply to the world of the text, everything functions at a premium.[8]

These elevated premiums, or perceived values, include social characteristics like honor, personal attributes including beauty and health, societal traits including economic and financial matters, and even the production of commodities such as the favorable weather that nurtures agrarian life. Furthermore, this concept applies to population numbers. A modern worldview would perceive the world's population as being in unlimited and at times excessive supply. On the other hand, in the world of Scripture, people suffered shortened average life spans due to malnourishment, malnutrition, unsafe birthing processes, inadequate medicine, and unsanitary conditions. All of these led to overall poor health, which resulted in a depleted life span. This perpetuated the association of the limited good concept with human population. The impact was that this view of limited supply was reinforced throughout all things that mattered in life.

The Holy Spirit as a Limited Good

The limited good worldview applies also to the Spirit of God. In the world of Scripture, this entity was viewed as being short in supply and high in demand. Ezekiel 10 records the Spirit of God withdrawing from the temple, which then leads to the Spirit's extended absence. As noted previously, the Holy Spirit is conspicuously absent from corresponding texts in the Second Temple era, and the record is absent of any substantial indication that the Spirit ever returned to that temple.

8. Neyrey, "Limited Good," 103–6.

CHAPTER 10: FATHER, SON, AND SPIRIT

Furthermore, the Spirit was strongly associated with prophecy. By the first century, prophetic speech became viewed as being diminished (in most optimistic terms) and by some, in more prominent and pessimistic terms, as being totally abolished.[9] Because of the view that prophetic speech had been eradicated, it is unsurprising that many apocryphal and pseudo texts of the Second Temple era appeal to previous traditions and characters rather than leaning on their contemporaries, because the belief was the Spirit as an agent of prophecy was far more authoritative and active in previous generations. Additionally, some contend that evidence of the eroding prophetic voice is already found in the later prophetic traditions of the Old Testament.[10]

Purity as a Limited Good

The implications of the supposed disappearance of the Holy Spirit were extraordinarily profound. The Spirit of God was connected not only with prophetic utterance, but also with purity.[11] Given this, as social conditions became more tainted, it was expected that the Spirit would be in less operation. Likewise, but alternatively, as the instances of the Spirit are reduced, increased impurities are the result. Mary Douglas establishes that among minority societies like that of ancient Israel, purity was correlated to the physical orifices of the body.[12] Accordingly, Hebrew law concerns itself with what enters and exits the physical body. Examples include food, menstruation, childbirth, and circumcision. In addition, legal restrictions existed for those with specific blemishes, including of the orifices, enumerating restrictions regarding the blind, deaf, and mute. Skin impairments, often articulated as leprosy within biblical tradition, were seen as a particularly heinous defilement of the bodily, since sores essentially generated new orifices, which meant the body in entirety became such an entry and exit point of impurities including dirt, infection, and disease.

Moreover, in such cultures, regulations regarding the bodily orifices became a surrogate for the communal, social orifices. Ancient Israel as a sub-society was distinctly concerned with controlling the social gateways and monitoring those who entered and exited the collective. The further

---

9. Hill, *New Testament Prophecy*, 21.
10. Hill, *New Testament Prophecy*, 21.
11. Keener, *Spirit in the Gospels*, 9.
12. Douglas, *Purity and Danger*, 144.

their social boundaries were threatened, the tighter their restrictions became. As little as is known of the Pharisees, Luke-Acts record the sect was seeking to tighten social borders. These concerns were not unique in first-century Judaism. Other subcultures were noted to tighten their social gateways, including the Essenes at Qumran, who viewed their community as the feasible alternative to a society permeated with uncleanliness, and considered isolation preferable to and perhaps a remedy for impurity. The reason why, in part, is a belief that the Spirit of God, the agent of purity, was a diminished limited good. Since purity correlated to the bodily orifices, it is symbolic that prophetic speech, forthcoming from the body's most visible orifice, was disrupted.

The concerns of these representative groups (Pharisees, Essenes, and others) were quite relevant. What other factors would threaten societal orifices, creating impurities? To some, these would include the loss of language and culture, which Jewish Palestine fell victim to as diverse languages were spoken, and Hellenism had made its way through the "gateways" following a series of imperial impositions. In the first-century setting, Rome's influence was considered a pollution of sacred land not only because it controlled the region, but also because the empire introduced images and ideology promoting and proselytizing "Roman imperial theology."[13]

In some places, the vast majority of land, commodities, and money were considered tainted, being controlled by non-Jews and flowing out of the sacred land into the hands of either Rome, its operatives, or clients. What was supposed to be the holiest location, the temple, and its most sacred sect, the priests, had become defiled being subject to the patronage of Rome and Rome's client kings of the Herodian dynasty. All of this indicated that purity itself would have been viewed, consciously or unconsciously, as a limited good.

Purification by Water and Spirit

How is such a situation remedied? How does one purify self, or more importantly the community and corporate organizations and operations? How can sins be forgiven while a perpetual state of impurity persists? It was a formidable task that would require a collective cleansing of the entire social setting.

---

13. This is a term coined by Crossan, "Roman Imperial Theology," loc. 796.

CHAPTER 10: FATHER, SON, AND SPIRIT

John the Baptizer washed people for the forgiveness of sins, an important but simultaneously mysterious entity even within modern Christian traditions. However, as effective as he was, he was limited, in part, by his stationary posture attached to the Jordan River, as well as being restricted to baptizing one or perhaps a few people at a time. However, John the Baptist refers to the one who is greater, whose baptism will be widespread, and of the Holy Spirit and fire. Scholars have debated the meaning of fire in this context; however, in this usage, fire is purifying rather than punitive.

While water baptism is distinct from Spirit baptism, they are connected, with evidence attesting that the act of water is a signpost for that of the Spirit. Acts 1:5 says, "John baptized with water . . . but in a few days from now you will be baptized with the holy spirit." The indication is what John did, Jesus will do in greater measure; and what had come to be viewed as a limited good is now distributed liberally. In this way, God's good *epangelia* ("promise," "gift") or currency becomes available. Curiously, in one of the two instances where *epangelia* is used in the Septuagint in Amos 9:6, it deviates from the Hebrew text, and the accompanying language is that God pours water out over the earth. The context is a picture of exile that turns to reinstatement as Amos 9:11–15 is one of the most beautiful pictures of restoration in all Scripture. This unique echo of *epangelia* by Luke is consistent with his authorial design and features, and he uses Amos to highlight the restoration that would take place in Acts.

The Holy Spirit as God's Commodity

Therefore, the Holy Spirit outpouring in Acts is the currency or commodity that generates a unique patron-client relationship between God and the Spirit recipients. The Spirit imagery of water and fire as a purification agent, that curiously in Luke-Acts leads all the way to Rome at the conclusion of the Acts narrative, is an important adjacent topic; but, interestingly enough, it reads as if the entire purpose was to get this patronage to Rome. Nevertheless, the Spirit of purity is also connected to prophetic speech. Luke declares that prophecy has been restored in Peter's quotation of Joel in his Acts 2 sermon. Luke incorporates widespread evidence of the restoration of prophecy; brief but potent examples come from Luke 1, the introduction to his entire corpus. In Luke 1:41–42, Elizabeth is noted to be filled with the Spirit and speaks "blessed art thou among women." Mary was informed that the Spirit would come upon her (1:35) and then she speaks her Magnificat in 1:46–55. Zechariah's Benedictus (1:68–79) comes only after he is noted to be filled with the Spirit in 1:67. The examples of this in Luke-Acts are extensive; however, one need not read beyond Luke 1 to find strong evidence arguing that prophecy has returned resulting from the Spirit.

New Temple Theology and the Holy Spirit's Abundance

The final portion of this section on the Holy Spirit treats the matter of new temple theology in Luke-Acts. On the heels of what has already been referenced, whereas Second Temple Judaism lacks a clear attestation of God's Spirit returning to the temple, the highlight of early Acts is the separation from the Jerusalem temple. Luke's Gospel is structured on a lengthy narrative toward Jerusalem, while, after Stephen's speech in Acts 7 regarding the temple, the narrative then flows outward. The Ten Degrees of Holiness from the Mishnaic tradition offers a useful picture of sacred real estate within earlier Jewish tradition. Matters of purity flowed toward Jerusalem, to the Temple Mount, the temple courts, eventually to the Holy of Holies. However, with the Spirit's arrival in Acts 2, there is not only a parallel to God's Spirit descending at the tabernacle and first temple dedication, but the tongues of fire echoes temple imagery from the 1 Enoch 14:9–22. Hence, with the Spirit's arrival, the new temple is established, and the forgiveness of sin, formerly reserved to the temple cult in Jerusalem, becomes accessible.

Whereas Jerusalem temple theology saw purity flowing toward the sacred city and holy temple, as all roads led inward, in contrast, the purity flow in Acts is external, moving from Jerusalem toward Samaria as part of the "uttermost," a clear outward flow. The new temple of Luke-Acts, the Holy Spirit–indwelled church, is superior, not only in its mobility, a hallmark feature to the Lukan narratives and a shared motif with the earlier tabernacle, but also that, unlike the former temple, the new temple is able to transfer purity, whereby the former location could not transmit purity but could be defiled, the superior assets of the new temple enable the movement to transmit purity to the ends of the earth (Acts 1:8).

The impact, once more, in a limited good society, is that when something is depleted, such as the Holy Spirit, it is expected to be forever lost. One of the great theological beauties of Luke-Acts is the liberal disbursement of the Holy Spirit, which established the currency of patronage between God and the client church. The Jews are bestowed the Spirit at Pentecost in Acts 2, then the Samaritans in Acts 8, and finally the gentiles in Acts 10. The Spirit as God's gift is an important feature of each narrative.

God's Patron-Client Brokers

Within this patronage model, brokers assist in connecting persons and groups to God's Spirit. One of the two clearest attestations of this is found in John the Baptist, who, in a sense, brokers both of God's great gifts in Jesus and the Holy Spirit. It was at John's baptism that the Spirit descended on Jesus as a dove. While this requires further treatment, it is worth considering how this event fits into the model. The second obvious brokerage connection is found in the apostolic group who become a principal conduit for the Spirit's dispersion.

Consider the Samaritan Pentecost of Acts 8. The Holy Spirit reception in this case required the presence and activity of Peter and John, a clear indication of brokerage. Furthermore, in Acts 10, the critical moment of Spirit empowerment of Cornelius's household requires Peter's presence and endorsement. In Acts 9, Ananias is a broker of sorts to Saul of Tarsus. Of course, Saul himself seems to have become a broker. Other participants with a less clear role include Barnabas, Silas, Stephen, and Philip all having interesting functions; albeit there is a clear distinction between Philip versus Peter and John in Samaria, whose presence is required for the Holy Spirit outpouring. Another aspect is that Jesus, as a Son, has a vested interest in the Father's share of profit, not as a mere subordinate but as an heir or partner. Furthermore, Jesus's role in the supply of the Spirit is also critical.

The Early Church as a Client

Furthermore, the church or recipients of the Spirit are the client in this model. The implications of that assertion are profound. For any client in a patronage system, reciprocity is of extreme import. Within collectivistic society, reciprocity was not merely an expectation but a requirement to maintain relationships. Every action extended from one person to another required some response. Failure to appropriately reciprocate resulted in the dissolution of relationships. The individual who failed to reciprocate would be shamed, and the individual who did not receive fair reciprocity would be dishonored. The greatest social currency of the Mediterranean world was the measurement of honor (contrasted with shame) since it determined virtually all aspects of life. John Barclay's remarkable work treating grace or gifts as an instrument of reciprocity is not only well established in historical and linguistic argument, but is conceptually applicable indicating required behavior, especially when receiving the *epangelia ho patēr*.[14] In other words, *charis* is but one of many expressions from the ancient world that generated reciprocal obligations.

Reciprocal Obligations of the Church

The intriguing dilemma that is presented is how the church is to appropriately reciprocate. Patronage relationships were built on inequitable power standings; therefore, a client was not positioned to reciprocate in kind. Likewise, a good theological statement the church might proclaim is that reciprocity is not about earning God's gifts; rather, the commodity is something the church cannot repay. However, what was required of clients in antiquity and the church contemporary is appropriate reciprocity.

Socio-Economic Ethics of the New Temple Paradigm

The first of two primary ways and means that Luke expresses acceptable reciprocity for God's gifts is the participation in a series of socio-economic ethics. To this, Jesus, in Luke 19:13, leaning on the context of the parable of the shrewd manager (Luke 19:1–9), a story regarding patronage relations, states that "no man can serve two masters" to distinguish patronage to God in juxtaposition to that of money. The introduction to Jesus's ministry is John the Baptist's witness in Luke 3; the crowd requested regarding their reciprocal obligation, to which he communicated a series of ethics. Those with excess are to share, and those with power, abstain from exploitation. Additionally, Luke's Sermon on the Plain (Luke 6), which parallels and contrasts from the Matthean tradition, specifically draws out further socio-economic implications. Luke's examples of socio-economic ethics are well attested, to table fellowship, forgiveness, and self-surrender. Perhaps the most intriguing instance of failed and successful patronage and reciprocity in the Lukan tradition comes in the contrast figures of the rich ruler

---

14. Barclay, *Paul and the Gift*.

CHAPTER 10: FATHER, SON, AND SPIRIT

(Luke 18) and the positive example of Zacchaeus (Luke 19). The church then modeled these ethics, attested throughout Acts.

Offering Glory and Praise to God as Patron

The second highlighted reciprocal aspect of patronage in antiquity is that clients would affirm and bestow glory, honor, and praise upon their patrons. Is this not what Christian worship is—recognizing how the God of history maneuvers through his many mighty acts? From this comes many considerations for practical theology, studies in worship and liturgy. This matter of worship, particularly corporate worship, which in collectivistic societies was an imperative, becomes an integral part of reciprocity in the contemporary context even. Therefore, matters of church membership, attendance, relationship, cooperation, and collaboration within the worship community should be considered not in a self-serving fashion but holy dedication. When a congregation meets for worship, and even in gatherings such as academic conferences, believers are not only continuing this patronage model, but also participating in reciprocity in response to God's good gifts.

Chapter 11: Inspired Meals in Luke-Acts

Food and Table Fellowship as a Means of Grace[1]

A First-Century Understanding of Grace

JOHN M. G. BARCLAY'S WRITINGS from the most recent decade have challenged New Testament scholars to reconsider and explore the various contexts of grace from a first-century Mediterranean perspective, rather than by means of a seventeenth-century Lutheran position.[2] Barclay's findings did not catch lexicographers by surprise, as χάρις (*charis*) encompasses a multitude of connotations, including "favorable attitude toward someone or something";[3] "gratitude; esteem";[4] "beauty, charm, favor, goodwill, free benevolence, gift, benefit, gratitude";[5] "favor, gift, thanks";[6] "charm, beauty, glory, success, respect, honor, favor, benefit, votive gift, thank-offering, gift, pleasure, joy, favor, grace, kindness, partiality, influence, allure, favor, gratitude, thankfulness."[7] The *TDNT*, like the *BrillDAG*, includes a much broader base of usages for χάρις, as both resources offer a comprehensive explanation that extends across various periods and genres.[8] Assuredly, the connotations of "grace" are more deep and complex than the isolated meaning to which some modern Christian traditions have confined it. Within

---

1. This paper was first read at Wesleyan Theological Society Trevecca Nazarene University (Nashville, Tennessee) on March 1, 2024.
2. Barclay, *Paul and the Gift*; see also Barclay, *Paul and the Power of Grace*.
3. Louw and Nida, *Greek-English Lexicon*, 298.
4. Balz and Schneider, *Exegetical Dictionary*, 3:457.
5. Spicq and Ernest, *Theological Lexicon*, 500.
6. Silva, *NIDNTTE*, 653.
7. Montanari, *BrillDAG*, see entry for "χάρις."
8. Conzelmann and Zimmerli, *TDNT*, 375.

the context of the New Testament, χάρις was a currency of the relational aspects of patrons and clients, soliciting reciprocity.[9]

Properly understood and applied within its context, biblical grace occurs when relationships, both personal and corporate, are extended by God, and it involves reciprocity through which each party involved will benefit. This is a broad concept. In the early church's context, grace flows when God extends general goodness toward the people; and likewise, reciprocity is observed when the church receives these gifts and responds with gratitude, worship, and conduct in accordance with the divine plan. Therefore, within this chapter, grace is addressed in Luke-Acts within this conceptual framework of mutual benefit. The study will highlight instances describing food and meals when the operation of grace is evident, even where the exact language of χάρις may not be supplied in the text.[10]

Survey of Meals and Food in Acts

This section will first examine eight references to food and meals in Acts, with positive, grace-filled attestations followed by a brief consideration of two antithetical stories with a negative narrative framework where grace is absent.

Direct References to Food in Acts

Food Sharing in Acts 2:46

> *Every day they continued to gather together by common consent in the temple courts, breaking bread from house to house, sharing their food with glad and humble hearts. (Acts 2:46)*

The initial reference to meals in Acts follows the programmatic events associated with Pentecost in Acts 2, remarked upon in the concluding summary of the day. Immediately preceding his ascension, Jesus expressed to his disciples the power they would receive from the Holy Spirit enabling their witness (Acts 1:8). Upon the Holy Spirit's engagement with this disciple group in Acts 2, speech becomes an integral part of this witness. Peter clarifies the

---

9. Malina, "Grace/Favor," 77. See also Barclay, *Paul and the Gift*, 29, 25.

10. Barclay clarifies that the same concept extends to other New Testament writers, not just Luke—that using alternate words for grace still conveys the identical concept as grace and reciprocity. See Barclay, "Paul and the Gift" (webinar).

gospel testimony by articulating that he and those who took part in the upper room gatherings were in the process of experiencing the fulfillment of Joel's prophecies (Acts 2:16–21). Moreover, Peter addresses the Jerusalem crowd with a testimony concerning Jesus. This crowd of listeners consisted of locals and pilgrims who had gathered for the festival events of the recent Passover week. During that time Jesus, whose ministry had been confirmed by accompanying signs, had been handed over to the gentile rulers for judgment and crucifixion (Acts 2:22–23). However, God validated him by raising him from the dead, and Jesus now remains active as Lord and Christ post-ascension (Acts 2:24). Peter then gives a reinterpretation of scripture when quoting from the Davidic psalms to give authoritative precedent for resurrection belief (2:25–36).

Upon hearing the Petrine message, gatherers were compelled to ask, "What should we do?" (2:37) to which Peter responds that the correct reaction is repentance for their sin of rejection, baptism as a means of demonstrating their repentance (which would become an initiation rite), and reception of the Holy Spirit that would be granted to them (Acts 2:38). Peter's speech includes two critical components that are inclusive and egalitarian, and that in many ways echo Jesus's table ethics in the Gospel. First, according to Joel's prophecy, the Holy Spirit's accessibility transcends traditional lines of social demarcation including gender, age, and the class distinction between slaves and free people (Acts 2:17–18). Moreover, Peter's own commentary of the event expresses the accessibility of the experience not only to his listeners, but also to their children and "all who are far away" (Acts 2:39). Such a universal tone is reminiscent of the undercurrent of Jesus's controversial manners regarding table fellowship in the Gospel. In addition, it signals the inclusive early engagement of the believers in Acts, accepting the return of exiles and demonstrating grace.

Immediately following Peter's speech, a summary of events associated with the newly formed group is provided (Acts 2:42–47), here food is included in the very first description of the early church. In Acts 2:41, Luke records that on that day of Pentecost, three thousand new disciples were added to the one hundred twenty disciples from the upper room experience. These are hallmarked by their devotion to teaching and fellowship, to prayer, and to "the breaking of bread" (Acts 2:42).[11] This is a clear mention of meals that is followed by the liquidation of property for

---

11. Luke Timothy Johnson affirms that this includes both ordinary and sacramental meals; see Johnson, *Acts*, 58.

distribution to those with needs (2:45). While this distribution does not directly describe the purchase of food as part of the use of the proceeds, the likelihood is that in a world where the vast majority of persons existed at near subsistence levels, and where food was a politicized phenomenon, the distribution either primarily or in part consisted of food.[12] Moreover, in addition to their worship and love, Luke reemphasizes that the early church members were "breaking bread from house to house, sharing their food" (Acts 2:46).[13] This reinforcement in both the initial description in verse 42 and again in verse 46 indicates that the sharing of food comprised a considerable part of their identity.

In this initial depiction of the early church, references to food are overt. However, while grace is not directly mentioned, it is clearly inferred as its signs are apparent. Grace is evident through the bestowing of benefits and favor, and the text is saturated with such descriptions. Not only are the prophets' theological representations of God's promises fulfilled, but salvation, Holy Spirit baptism, and the constitution of the early church into a household structure are unquestionably conveyed as mechanisms from God.[14] Additionally, other signs of favor and grace were included in the practice of the early church, wherein the "miraculous signs" no doubt indicated benefits for the recipients. The distribution of goods is also a sign and means of giving, and the food itself was shared. Undoubtedly, within this first scene with a double reference to table fellowship, meals and grace converge.

Feeding the Widows in Acts 6:1–7

> *Their widows were being overlooked in the daily distribution of food.*
> *(Acts 6:1b)*

---

12. Christopher Hays connects the events in verse 45 to the meals for the needy. Verse 45 flows into verse 46 where meals are reinforced. See Hays, *Luke's Wealth Ethics*, 193.

13. William Larkin asserts that the early group, with some regularity, would have converged ordinary meals with taking of the sacrament. If this is presumed true, it emphasizes the early church's experience of table fellowship as an inspired time; see Larkin, *Acts*, 62.

14. David deSilva affirms the early church in the New Testament functioned as an organization of a household, which provided benefits to the familial relationships in a much more gracious way than routine social constructs; see deSilva, *Honor, Patronage, Kinship and Purity*, 198–99.

The next direct reference to food in Acts occurs with an internal dispute. In keeping with the Torah (Exod 22:22–27), the growing group of early Christian believers were taking responsibility for the care of widows, which included distributing food daily (Acts 6:2). The mention of food here is clear. The distribution is from the generosity of individuals and possibly a collection from those who gave in Acts 2:45, which also transmits the idea of grace. Moreover, this being noted as a daily occurrence established the high degree of need for many demographics during this period, but also the effective supply of the early church in terms of sacrifice of the early church in meeting the demanding needs.

As with Ananias and Sapphira in the previous chapter (5:1–11), when the church is gaining momentum, suddenly a narrative problem arises. The precise complaint of these widows is uncertain, nor is the legitimacy of their complaint validated. However, whether it be a problem of perception or fact, the issues demand to be addressed. The most likely scenario is that these are diasporic widows who have relocated to the region of Jerusalem due to burial arrangements made for their late husbands in the land of ancestry, and they remain awaiting their own eventual burial.[15] If this were the case, it would explain not only why these widows were so vulnerable, without the security of longstanding familial and social relationships close by to provide care for them, but also why the social issue arose, given the potential dichotomy between the diasporic families and those who remained natives.

The remedy is that the apostles elected to appoint seven deacons to administer the food. Grace is present in this scene, not only that men are selected who are "full of Spirit and wisdom," but also in that these seven appear with Hellenistic names.[16] It is reasonable to expect that those responsible for equitable distribution would be representatives of the group bringing the complaint, which would be remarkable evidence of the grace that was present. Two of these deacons, Stephen and Philip, are remarked upon as having specific graces resting upon them which lead them into functioning as effective and critical gospel witnesses.

Moreover, this small pericope is sandwiched between other hallmarks of grace. First, in Acts 5:33, the temple rulers desire to execute Peter and John. To the benefit of these two apostles, and more so, that of the rulers, cooler heads prevail when Gamaliel rises to give a balanced perspective, a

---

15. Keener, *Acts*, 2:1268.
16. Keener, *Acts*, 2:1287.

CHAPTER 11: INSPIRED MEALS IN LUKE-ACTS

working of grace. Additionally, at the conclusion of that narrative, although the apostles are beaten, yet grace is present as they rejoice in their worthiness to suffer, and in their courage to maintain their preaching testimony. Furthermore, in Acts 6:7 just after the apostles pray for the seven deacons, the grace of God again prevails. The result is not only that another potential disruption of unity is handled, but also that the word of God spreads, disciples increase greatly, and witness is expressed even to the priests whose superiors had just been at odds with the apostles. Once again, near the mention of food in Acts, the activity of grace takes place, and, specifically, God's grace is convincing. Whether the author creates a relationship between the food and grace by design is uncertain; however, the connection is present.

Saul of Tarsus in Acts 9:1–22

After taking some food, his strength returned. (Acts 9:19)

The next treatment of meals in Acts is connected to Saul and his response to the Christological event on the road to Damascus. Whether that moment indicates a conversion or a calling for Saul is secondary to this investigation. From Luke's record, Saul was present at the stoning of Stephen (Acts 7:58). The author's description of the cloaks being laid at Saul's feet is imagery that evokes a juxtaposition with the image of Barnabas bringing money to the apostles and laying it at their feet (Acts 4:34–37). Accordingly, in a sense, Saul becomes the personification of persecution, not only since he is present at Stephen's stoning, but also as the primary culprit in what Luke depicts as a wave of resistance that begins to push early believers out of Jerusalem (Acts 8:1–2).

The familiar narrative of Saul's meeting with Jesus is set on the road to Damascus, where, after receiving the priest's approval in Jerusalem, he seeks to arrest more believers. On his travels, Saul is confronted with a light and the voice of Jesus, which create a blindness. Luke notes that for three days, while he could not see, he "neither ate nor drank anything" (Acts 9:9). Clearly, since the inclusion of that detail is of no historical import, food is mentioned because it serves a vital function in the narrative. Whereas throughout Luke's Gospel and then in Acts, meals served as a signpost for grace, union, and Christological happening, Saul's lack of meals is tied to the idea that he is absent of grace up to this point.

Meanwhile, Ananias is also confronted with the Lord. He is told to go to Saul and lay hands on him to restore his eyesight. At Ananias's hesitation, the voice informs him of the nature of Saul's calling. When Ananias meets Saul, he lays hands on him, vision is restored, Holy Spirit filling occurs, and water baptism happens; and, most critical to the purposes of this chapter, he eats (Acts 9:19). The account is specific enough to evidence the change of Saul's posture from the apparent abstinence from food, regardless of the motivations, to his reception of food, enabling his strength to return.

The grace from God is also visible in this portion of the story. The risen Jesus interrupts Saul from further incriminating himself with the church and provides him with a holy vocation as an alternate. He is commissioned with a unique and integral task in the early church, given the Holy Spirit, initiated into the church at baptism, and his sight returns. Moreover, Saul becomes the first human voice within the Lukan corpus to identify Jesus positively as the Son of God, prompting the amazement of the people (Acts 9:20). This amazement is a key response that Luke employs, notably to indicate the operation of Jesus in the Gospel.

Not only is grace depicted in the details above, but within the same chapter, Saul is remarkably able to exit Damascus without harm (Acts 9:23–24). He then travels to Jerusalem, where he gains an advocate in Barnabas, who assists in the apostolic reception (9:26–31). In the narrative flow, Paul begins to travel soon afterward, demonstrating mirror miracles not only to Peter but to Jesus, as a sign of grace afforded to him.

Cornelius in Acts 10:1—11:18

He became hungry and wanted to eat, but while they were preparing the meal, a trance came over him. (Acts 10:10)

The next event where food and meals overlap the concept of grace occurs with Peter's visit to Cornelius. In a vision, a messenger from God conveys to Cornelius that God acknowledges him because of his prayers and "acts of charity." Thus, early in the narrative, the conceptuality of grace being extended by God is described in response to Cornelius's acts of grace. Moreover, his giving charity could reasonably have been expected to have consisted of providing persons in need with meals, either by giving food directly or by granting money to provide food indirectly. For those in need in ancient times, meals were a primary source of charity since money was less relied upon than tangible goods.[17]

17. For instance, the parable of the lost coin (Luke 15:8–10) demonstrates the limited quantity of coins within the hands of those who are expected to be common

The next day, in the adjacent scene, Peter, while hungering and waiting on food, experiences a trance wherein he perceives a series of creatures considered unclean. Despite this, a voice instructs him to "slaughter and eat"; however, Peter contests this. Soon afterward, he is summoned to Cornelius. To reiterate, the subject of food is connected to the various defiled, or formerly considered defiled, creatures that Peter is either metaphorically or told to go and eat. Since Cornelius was a gentile, he and his home would have likewise been considered defiled according to many Second Temple Jews.[18] Despite this, due to the message from the trance, Peter is confident enough to enter Cornelius's home, an action which would be contrary to purity guidelines according to many or most of Peter's Jewish counterparts.

Herein multiple streams of grace manifest, not only toward Peter, but also and even more significantly to Cornelius, who receives the benefit of engaging with the apostle directly. For Cornelius and his family, the evidence of favor is the reception of the Holy Spirit, baptism into the church, and acknowledgment that they have been incorporated into the movement begun by Jesus. This scene presents an integral narrative redirection with crucial theological development as Peter subsequently returns to Jerusalem and gives an account of his trance, which employed the rich metaphoric imagery of meal habits as a mechanism to transfer grace.

While no specific record of sharing food is detailed in Peter's encounter with Cornelius, one must suspect that Cornelius was hospitably oriented given the cultural emphasis of his day. In keeping with his charitable affirmation, it is reasonable to expect that he would have offered table fellowship to Peter. Some have debated whether Peter would have eaten unclean food with Cornelius, but this argument is secondary to the focus of this chapter. It is reasonable to presume, based on the trajectory of the story and his vision, that Peter would have accepted an offer of table fellowship whether he would have partaken of unclean food, which remains a possibility. The evidence of grace is abundant in the scene, and the usage of food as a chief metaphor is an integral part of Acts. Moreover, readers familiar with the culture of the biblical text would assume that table

---

individuals. For those who existed beneath subsistence, accessibility to coins would have been more limited.

18. Moreover, the fact that he was a centurion ascribes to him further degrees of profanity since he was an imperial representative. Although Luke appreciates and gives honor to the character, the broader populace of first-century Jewish Palestine would have considered association with such a person cause to make one severely tainted.

fellowship was made. Hence again, these two features, table fellowship and signs of grace, significantly overlap within this section.

The Antioch Christians and Famine (Acts 11:19–30)

> Now it was in Antioch that the disciples were first called Christians.... Agabus got up and predicted by the Spirit that a severe famine was about to come over the whole inhabited world. (This took place during the reign of Claudius). So the disciples, each in accordance with his financial ability, decided to send relief to the brothers living in Judea. (Acts 11:26, 28b–29)

Following Cornelius's Holy Spirit reception, the narrative of Acts flows more broadly into the broader Mediterranean world. Acts 11:19–27 records the emergence of the church in Antioch, one that would become an early hub of Christian activity as well as a launching site for the Pauline ministry. Within the narrative, grace is flowing on the heels of the gospel having reached the gentiles, by way of a centurion, nonetheless. In Acts 11:27 "the hand of the Lord was upon them," while in verse 23, "they saw the grace of God," and "rejoiced" because of the "devoted hearts."

Within that same section, groups coming to faith offer multiple attestations demonstrating evidence of grace in operation. Moreover, Luke records that they were first called Christians at that time (11:26). Scholars have considered many questions relating to this assertion. Some doubt the historicity of the remark, given that the inscription "Christian" does not appear anywhere else until the late first century.[19] Others speculate that it was a negative connotation, ascribed to the church by skeptics.[20] However, verse 26 says "the disciples *were* first *called* Christians" (emphasis mine), and here the Greek for "called," χρηματίζω (chrēmatizō), although used sparsely in New Testament writings, tends to denote inspired speech.[21] Additionally, the lexical examination of the broader usage of *chrēmatizō* also denotes oracles. Although some scholars tend to be skeptical of the prophetic designation of the term, the very next verse (11:27) indicates prophets appearing in Antioch, offering validation the connection to inspired speech and providing affirmation to the title "Christian." If this point is correct, then grace

---

19. Keener, *Acts*, 2:1848–50.
20. Keener, *Acts*, 2:1848–50.
21. Montanari, *BrillDAG*, see entry for "χρηματίζω."

is operating with such a regard in Antioch that it is there when the prophetic label of Christian becomes attached to the church.

These prophets express other critical components in their message in 11:27–30. Agabus asserts that a coming famine would affect the broader Mediterranean world. In a setting where most people existed at subsistence levels, hardly any reserves could be relied upon to feed people during widespread and prolonged famines. As already evidenced in Acts, certain segments of the population, specifically the widows in Judea, are already dependent upon the generosity of others for their meals. Furthermore, the inference from Acts 2:42–46 and 4:32–35 is that food distribution was prominent among the early apostolic group. Given these factors, and in anticipation of the upcoming famine, the Christians in Antioch decide to make a sacrifice by offering provisions to send to the churches in Judea. The indication is that because of the prophets' words, these disciples can begin to secure food or means before the famine strikes. This is once again a demonstration of present grace displayed through the giving of these early Christians. Moreover, this grace not only overlaps with the idea of meals but is directly associated with food supply.

The Philippian Jailer in Acts 16:34

> *The jailer brought them into his house and set food before them, and he rejoiced greatly that he had come to believe in God, together with his entire household. (Acts 16:34)*

The literary center of Acts records the Jerusalem Council in Acts 15, which conveys a crucial event in the development of the early church. During this event, a conscious effort is made to secure uncircumcised gentile believers into the church. Following this occasion, Paul, Silas, and Timothy set out once again to resume missionary journeys.

Acts 16:6–10 then records Paul's dream of a Macedonian man who solicits him to cross into that region. This is of both geographical and cultural importance. As Paul heeded that call, from a contemporary vantage point, he was crossing from the region of Asia (minor) into Europe. Some have speculated that the man of this vision was Alexander the Great, reasoning that he intended to unite East and West, and that Paul's gospel mission is now seeking to accomplish the same goal.[22] Regardless of the identity of the

---

22. Keener, *Acts*, 3:2343.

character in the dream, the certainty remains that gospel transmission progresses farther into critical portions of the world. It draws closer to Rome and engages the region of ancient Greece, a pivotal point in Mediterranean history. Unmistakably, grace, or God's favor, continues to be demonstrated as the gospel reaches new lands.

The initial key event in this region occurs at Philippi. This city was a strategic location, a Roman colony filled with retired soldiers in a setting that very much resembled Rome. There, Paul encounters Lydia and an unnamed slave girl who suffers from a "spirit of divination." Paul casts the spirit out of her, which provokes the anger of her owners who are rendered unable to continue to exploit and profit from her. This action results in Paul and Silas being put into jail after being beaten. Around midnight, Paul and Silas, obviously benefiting from God's grace, are praising God and singing when an earthquake affects the structure, permitting prisoners to escape. The guard determines to take his own life so that he might die in a more honorable fashion than an execution for failing to commandeer his prisoners. However, Paul thwarts the officer's attempt, informing him that his prisoners remain. This prompts the jailer to then call upon the Lord for salvation.

The scene at the jail is so pertinent, not only as the gospel has moved into a new location, but also because this jailer, an agent of the state, is converted along with his household, all of whom are baptized that night. In an obvious way, grace is flowing within the text. However, in addition to the favor shown, the jailer brings Paul and Silas into his home. Here, the narrative offers another occasion of Jews entering the home of a gentile. In hospitality, the jailer provides them with food, attesting that, once again, when food is mentioned positively in Acts, it is in association with a critical transmission of grace. The jailer also treats Paul and Silas's wounds, and the next day both are released from jail with a public apology from the magistrate.

Paul and Eutychus in Acts 20:6–11

> *After he had broken bread and eaten, he talked with them a long time, until dawn. (Acts 20:11b)*

The subsequent scene of table fellowship occurs following an attestation of Paul's effectiveness in Ephesus, where the greatest demonstration of repentance occurs when the pagans of that community burn their highly valuable magic books, threatening to end the profession of idol-makers in that hub of pagan practice.

From there, Paul begins to retrace his steps backward toward Jerusalem, ushering in a significant literary narrative that will lead him through a series of controversies in that city. First, while Paul is in Troas teaching, a man named Eutychus falls asleep on a window ledge, plummeting three stories to his death. However, Paul functions as a conduit of healing for this young man who rises to life again. This encounter is significant. Resurrection is recorded by Luke only sparingly—twice through Jesus; then once through Peter, at the raising of Tabitha; and now, finally, through Paul as a mirror miracle. Plainly, the activity of raising a person from the dead is distinct from other healing miracles.

Even more significantly, this resurrection narrative is sandwiched between two instances involving food. The record describes the travelers breaking bread in Troas at the time of Paul's arrival and subsequent teaching. Additionally, following the raising of Eutychus, Luke notes in verse 11 that Paul returns to teach through the night until the dawn after "he had broken bread and eaten it" in a clear echo to Jesus's last supper in Jerusalem. The compounded narrative reinforces the importance of this meal sharing through its repeated reference to the breaking of bread. Concurrent with table fellowship, grace appears vibrantly within this text. The flow of favor is evident through Paul's arrival, through the fellowship and teaching, and climaxing with the resurrection of Eutychus from the dead.

Paul's Shipwreck in Acts 27:21–38

> Paul took bread and gave thanks to God in front of them all, broke it, and began to eat. So all of them were encouraged and took food themselves. (Acts 27:35–36)

The final occurrence in Acts that directly relates to grace with the partaking of food takes place during Paul's transit to Rome as he crosses the Mediterranean. Despite Paul having been in custody since his apprehension in Jerusalem, he desires to reach Rome to have an audience before the authorities there. Moreover, the overall geographical, literary, and theological flow of Acts anticipates this movement toward Rome. Therefore, rather than being filled with foreboding over his fate, Paul associates the trip with a sense of optimistic destiny. During their voyage, the ship encounters a violent storm, suffers damage, and is thrown off course for fourteen days. Luke records that as they fear for their lives, the passengers and crew lose their appetites.

Through a series of events and uncertainty, Paul eventually speaks to the crew and encourages them to eat. His speech is highly reminiscent of sacramental language. He took bread, broke it, and ate, then others followed and ate to satisfaction, a critical description of having plenty. Apparently, they ate enough that they were well satisfied and able to let go of the excess weight of additional wheat on the ship, throwing it into the sea. In a transparent way, the meal serves a key role in this event. This is compounded by the fact that the sailors' earlier refusal of food now transforms to an attitude of acquiescence and partaking with satisfaction.

The grace factor in this event is even more apparent. The next day, the ship reaches land, adding some security to the crisis. In addition, even as the soldiers determine to kill the prisoners to ensure none of them are lost, Paul convinces them of the detainees' compliance, saving them (recalling the earlier occasion where Paul and Silas voluntarily remain with the jailer in Philippi). This tale is accompanied by a clear indication of grace as the incarcerated and crew share a meal together and their lives are spared.

Negative References to Food and Meals in Acts

The examination of these eight direct references to food, meals, and table fellowship in Acts amply demonstrates that Luke employs positive reference to fellowship and meals in conjunction with affirming activity of God and his servants that is congruent to the concept of grace or favor. Next, it is necessary to consider instances where Luke depicts food negatively.

The Shipwreck in Acts 27:14–21

> *Since many of them had no desire to eat, Paul stood up among them and said, "Men, you should have listened to me and not put out to sea from Crete, thus avoiding this damage and loss." (Acts 27:21)*

Once such instance has already been referenced above in the story of the sea voyage. In this scene, the crew and passengers traveling on the voyage with Paul abstain from food during a time when the destiny of the ship and their personal fates were in peril. Noticeably, their lack of eating overlaps with their own uncertainty, thus connecting a negative experience with refraining from eating.

Herod Executes James in Acts 12:1–3

> *About that time King Herod laid hands on some from the church to harm them. He had James, the brother of John, executed with a sword. When he saw that this pleased the Jews, he proceeded to arrest Peter too. (This took place during the feast of Unleavened Bread.) (Acts 12:1–3)*

Acts 12 provides three additional examples of food connected to negative events. First, the inclusion of the feast of the Unleavened Bread in Luke's narrative links a food-related event with a negative occasion, the time when King Herod Agrippa has James executed, echoing Luke 22:1–6 when the rulers conspire against Jesus on that same occasion.

Moreover, Peter is also arrested by Agrippa I; and while Acts records his miraculous release from jail in Acts 12:3–19, some have suggested that Luke may have reordered events for literary purposes because Peter must remain alive until the Jerusalem Council in Acts 15, which is written outside of chronological sequence but in theological ordering.[23] The account of Peter's escape in Acts 12 contains compelling echoes of Jesus's resurrection, enjoining the reader to consider whether Peter himself has also been executed at some point, possibly following the execution of James. Following this instance of Peter's arrest and escape from prison in Acts 12, Peter is not mentioned again until the Council in Acts 15, marking his final appearance in the Lukan corpus.[24]

---

23. Wall, "Successors to 'the Twelve,'" 628–43.

24. To clarify, this writer tends to affirm a view wherein Peter's death is depicted within the symbolism correlated to Jesus's death and resurrection. This places him in the same standing with James, who is killed. Luke's reason for being unclear about the finality of Peter's life is because he intended the Jerusalem Council in Acts 15 to be at the literary center of the book and, therefore, could not convey Peter's death in Acts 12. The point of this section is to make Agrippa I more culpable of the negative events in Acts 12, including identifying him as Herod, linking him to his grandfather Herod the Great and his uncle Herod Antipas, even though Agrippa I's name was not actually Herod.

Herod Exploits Food Resources in Acts 12:3–21

> Now Herod was having an angry quarrel with the people of Tyre and Sidon . . . because their country's food supply was provided by the king's country. (Acts 12:20)

However, the concluding portion of the same chapter is even more pertinent, connecting food or eating with negative events twice, both with relation to Herod Agrippa I. Acts 12:20 connects Herod Agrippa with a controversy regarding food. Representatives from Tyre and Sidon have grown concerned that the king might use his control over the food supply for exploitative purposes.

Herod's Judgment in Acts 12:21–24

> Immediately an angel of the Lord struck Herod down because he did not give the glory to God, and he was eaten by worms and died. (Acts 12:23)

The very next remarks demonstrate that Herod, in a separate instance, stood before a crowd. In contrast to Peter and later Paul, who are eager to dismiss any insinuation that they might be gods in Acts, Herod Agrippa I permits himself to be described in deific manner. At that point, Luke records that Herod came under God's judgment, and is "struck" dead and is eaten by worms.

Luke has made three connections to consumption in Acts 12—first, the time marker of the Feast of Unleavened Bread; second, the complaints of the Tyrian and Sidonian representatives regarding Herod's control of the food supply; and third, the depiction of the worms that feed on Herod's body. In each of these three instances, the connection to food is negative. The first is a time of fasting from leaven; the second is connected to food shortage and controversy; and the third is grotesquely negative with Herod's corpse providing a feast for worms.

Likewise, these negative references to food are tied to events incongruent with grace in the story—the martyrdom of James and the arrest of Peter, the exploitation of food supplies, and Herod's acceptance of attributed divinity. Moreover, members of the Herodian dynasty are well situated within the Lukan corpus and in the social history of the Palestinian people; and here, Luke is juxtaposing the Herodians' corruption against the early church members' charitability. Accordingly, the negative reference to food consumption in both the famine with Agrippa's exploitation of Tyre and Sidon along with him being eaten by worms correlates with a clear attestation of the antithesis of grace, given Herod's actions and God's ensuing judgment.

Survey Results from Luke-Acts

The evidence of this study is that Luke deliberately portrays meals, food, and table fellowship as serving a critical function within the early church. These preliminary findings open the door to opportunities for further investigation, including ecclesiology. In what ways might the church consider these findings as having robust implications on all matters of table fellowship? Certainly, sacramental theology comes into deep conversation with these findings, not only Holy Communion but even general fellowship meals. Additionally, given the Roman control of general economics including the food supply of first century Palestine, one might consider the political implications of Luke's ethics toward food, generosity, and grace.

Chapter 12: The Gospel Message of Acts
The Good News to the Ends of the Earth

Introduction

THIS CHAPTER CONSIDERS THE meaning of "gospel" from the context of Acts, a unique genre from its New Testament counterparts as a book chronicling early church history, including the presentation of good news to an assortment of audiences. This project examines every presentation of Jesus within Acts, presuming these records of the early church to be gospel-worthy. The survey begins with the various presentations in Jerusalem, then considers the key expansion outside Palestine, and then the Pauline ministry throughout the Mediterranean world. This selection then presents a summary and synthesis of the findings. Before continuing, however, some limitations are noted, including that Acts represents but a single book with solo authorship; therefore its theological representation is limited. Additionally, its historical genre might be considered less adequate to construct and represent a totality of early Christian witness. However, one key assumption this writer operated within is that Acts presents ample data to make integral theological conclusions, sufficient for early audiences who may have had no other resources.

Gospel Transmission in Jerusalem

The gospel is delivered in extended detail in Jerusalem. Peter gives his well-known sermon on Pentecost, and then he addresses the temple three times, followed by Stephen's speech, the longest in the book of Acts, which precedes a transition to ministry outside Jerusalem.

CHAPTER 12: THE GOSPEL MESSAGE OF ACTS

Peter's Pentecost Sermon in Acts 2:14–41

Following the Holy Spirit's reception in the upper room, speech becomes a hallmark response to the event (2:1–13). It is on this occasion that Peter becomes the principal spokesman for this new movement. The setting is in Jerusalem; however, many pilgrims are present from the broader Mediterranean and Middle Eastern contexts. Although geographical diversity is represented, the gathering is one of ethnic Jews and possibly some gentile converts.

Peter's message is rooted within the Hebrew scriptural tradition. Initially, he explains the seemingly strange and diverse speech by connecting the Holy Spirit event to the prophecies of Joel 2. Peter's remarks, beginning with Joel, must be considered at least a portion of gospel transmission. Significantly, with the Spirit's offering, egalitarian speech is made available, with no respect for traditional barriers, including gender, age, or socioeconomic classes including slaves and free (2:14–21). The climax of Peter's quotation of Joel is that "everyone who calls on the name of the Lord will be saved," evidencing the accessibility of salvation (2:21).

Salvation within Luke-Acts is a broad topic referring to various events and types, wherein groups or individuals are granted some benefit, generally one that they themselves cannot provide, which makes them dependent of Jesus. The most prominent examples in Luke's Gospel include Jesus's healings; however, in Acts, this benefit takes on a twofold connotation, including the forgiveness of sin and the renewal of creation.[1] While Pentecost is the only time in the Lukan corpus that Joel's prophecies are directly referenced, the "good news" is identified through this connection as the continuation of Israel's story as depicted by the prophets. The words of God's spokesmen are being honored and coming to fulfillment. Therefore, understanding the gospel involves the assurance of the hope of God's commitment to Scripture.

Peter uses Joel as a segue to introduce Jesus, who is declared having validated his ministry with accompanying signs (2:22). Acts 2:23 introduces an integral and consistent part of the Jesus presentation—that he was given to be executed by the gentiles, albeit in alignment with God's purposes. However, 2:24 then affirms the resurrection, thereby expressing Jesus's superiority over death, by the hand of God.

---

1. For instance, Luke's Gospel employs "saved" when persons are restored to rightful societal positions (Luke 7:50, 19:9).

Peter then connects this event to the Davidic psalms. He demonstrates the development of Christological hermeneutics, wherein Israel's scriptures once more speak to the person of Jesus by way of David's affirmation that God would not abandon him in death. Peter directly reattaches David's first-person words to be a testament of Christ, again affirming the resurrection of Jesus and the dispersion of the Holy Spirit (2:25–36).

Just as the Petrine message reinforces the resurrection through connection with the Psalms and prophet Joel, it also expresses Jesus's ascension to the right hand of God as rooted within the Davidic writings.[2] Peter's purpose with this explanation is to incontrovertibly articulate the content of 2:36, that Jesus is both Lord and Christ. These two terms speak to Jesus being in authority—as Lord, in his ascension, and as Christ in the Messianic implications, validating him as the legitimate servant of God.

Reflecting on the Gospel at Pentecost

Peter's gospel transmission at Pentecost deliberately conveys several crucial points. First, Jesus is the fulfillment of Israel's prophecies. Second, being a man of God, he was handed over to be judged and crucified. However, third, God raised him from the dead; and now, fourth, Jesus occupies space at the right hand of God affirming his lordship and messianic standing. Fifth and finally, Jesus has dispatched the Holy Spirit in an egalitarian manner. These elements bear remembering as they will reappear throughout the evangelistic efforts in Acts.

Luke records the receptive crowd's response to Peter. They recognize their failure to honor Christ, and they ask what they must do (2:37). Peter affirms their need to repent (2:38); however, when calling on them to repent, Peter does not speak of converting from Judaism to Christianity, nor is he making a reference to abandoning the law of Torah and substituting it with grace, nor is he referring to a variety of general sins. Rather, he is calling them to specifically change their approach regarding Jesus. They must repent from their sin of rejection; they must be baptized, an act that had demonstrated repentance and cleansing under John the Baptizer and

---

2. The imagery of moving from the grave to the right hand of God as did Jesus also contains Old Testament parallels to Joseph in Genesis, who was placed in a pit by his brothers before eventually ascending to be Pharaoh's right hand. Also, Daniel was placed in a den of lions before he was vindicated by God and placed in power among the Persian ruling elite.

CHAPTER 12: THE GOSPEL MESSAGE OF ACTS

which will become an initiation rite into the church; and they will receive the Holy Spirit (2:38).

Once again, Peter affirms that the opportunity offered by the gospel message is accessible to all without limitation, available to as many as God will call (2:40–41). The result is that a significant group are baptized. In turn, they surrender their lives to become part of the church, contributing to the good of the community, partaking in fellowship, maintaining sacraments, and devoting themselves to the discipleship of teaching (2:42–47).

It is notable that Peter's presentation makes no mention of afterlife, whether heaven or hell, except for acknowledging Jesus's resurrection. Moreover, the isolated mention of sin refers to the context of the Jews' rejection of Jesus, with the hope that this sin would be forgiven as they reversed that error with the reception of the message. This initial sermon in Acts presents something of a programmatic model for apostolic preaching as recorded by Luke. It is not a primitive message yet to reach maturity; instead, it deliberately reflects a developed example of gospel transmission, even while being historically attached to the initial stages of church history and strategically placed within Jerusalem during a key socio-religious event.

Peter's First Temple Address (Acts 3:11–26)

The next gospel presentation occurs in the scene directly following Luke's Pentecost account. Acts 3:1–10 records Peter and John attending the Jerusalem temple for prayer. They both encounter a lame man who solicits alms, and in turn, they declare his healing by the authority of Jesus Christ. In response, the lame man becomes mobile. Upon recognizing this significant event, a crowd gathers to hear Peter's words. It is reasonable to assume that some of the audience may have already listened to Peter's address on Pentecost or heard a secondhand report, while others were first-time hearers of the good news shared by Peter.

Peter begins by affirming that Jesus is the one to credit for the lame man's healing, and he then offers an abbreviated synthesis of the Jesus story. The initial declaration is that God has "glorified his servant" (Acts 3:13), an inference of resurrection and ascension. Moreover, Peter remarks on the mistaken actions of those who rejected Jesus to the extent that he was handed over to Pilate for trial, and who manipulated circumstances to secure a guilty defendant to be released instead of Jesus. Peter refers to Jesus as the "Originator of life," raised from the dead, and declares himself and others as apostolic witnesses to these events. Again, Peter reinforces the authority of this Jesus as responsible for making the lame man well.

While the first portion of Peter's speech accounts for the misdeeds of the people, the second section conveys the standing of this crowd before God. In this address, the collective body of listeners, including their leaders, are considered ignorant in their actions and, in fact, have unknowingly been operating as agents of the fulfillment of the Messianic prophecies. Peter then provides the appropriate response for this crowd when he exhorts them to "repent and turn back" so that their "sins may be wiped out" (Acts 3:19). The context of "sins" referenced by Peter is their ignorant rejection of Jesus; therefore, the matter of repentance is directly related to that action.[3] Simply stated, in this case, repentance is the ideological antithesis of rejecting Jesus, so it entails altering one's stance from the rejection of Jesus to the embrace of Jesus.

The next element of Peter's speech refers to the effects that will proceed from embracing Jesus as Messiah. These include "times of refreshing" associated with the "presence of the Lord" and the initiation of the Messianic age (Acts 3:20). Peter continues remarking on the ascension as the intermediate time frame before a complete restoration. As he did in the Pentecost sermon, Peter roots the events of the Jesus story in Hebrew prophecy, and in that sense, the Christ event, as the fulfillment of prophecy, is the culmination of covenant history.[4] However, whereas Peter employed the Old Testament writings of the Psalms and Joel in the previous engagement, he now associates Jesus with Moses, Abraham, and the entire vein of prophetic lineage.

The most uniquely substantial material from this speech that adds value to this study comes from verse 23 contrasted with verses 25 and 26. First, Peter draws on the words of Moses from Deut 18:15 when he speaks in Acts 3:22 and 23. The latter portion of this reference in verse 23 engenders the idea of negative consequences for those who fail to obey the Mosaic-like prophet, when Peter says, "Every person who does not obey

---

3. Keener pulls together various references from Second Temple Jewish texts to argue that rejection of the "Lord was a terrible sin." This reinforces the assertion made here that the sins Peter references are concerning that rejection rather than a lifetime of law breaking. See Keener, *Acts*, 2:1092.

4. There are several Isaianic hints across this Petrine speech, further substantiating the Lukan product of Jesus as the fulfillment of the Hebrew prophet voices. See Keener, *Acts*, 2:1085.

CHAPTER 12: THE GOSPEL MESSAGE OF ACTS

that prophet will be destroyed and thus removed from the people"(Acts 3:23). Peter leaves the specifics undeveloped.

Regardless, this inclusion does provide an opportunity to consider Luke's intended teaching regarding negative implications for those who reject Jesus. However, modern readers should be careful not to presume an outright committal to a doctrine of hell from such a brief remark, as hell is not mentioned at all. Indeed, if listeners had been intended to draw on this judgment scenario to assume punishment even resembling the contemporary concept of hell, it would be expected that the punitive context would occupy an extended portion of Peter's presentation. Instead, this reference is placed as a near addendum of this temple speech, hardly the core of the message; and it is relevant that this insertion is completely absent from the model Pentecost sermon. In the overall quotation, Peter's focus is to identify Jesus as "an eschatological *prophet like* [Moses]' who reveals the plan of God and the way of God."[5]

Moreover, in the surrounding verses, Peter expresses a tone of reassurance, strongly emphasizing the benefits that those who receive Jesus may claim. According to the subsequent quote from Gen 22:18 in Acts 3:25, believers may lay claim to Abraham's blessing that "all the nations of the earth will be blessed." This indicates a blessing not only to the hearers but also to the nations as universal beneficiaries of the Jesus message.

Peter does not discuss the afterlife. The word *heaven* is used only in the context that heaven must receive Jesus "until the time all things are restored" (Acts 3:21). The restoration of "all things" carries the ideas of both physical body and broader creation and does not specifically denote placement in heaven as the salvation benefit. The language indicates not a rescue from earth, but the rescue of earth, by means of its renewal.

Finally, in Acts 3:26, Peter reemphasizes the resurrection of Jesus as a sign of repentance for those in Jerusalem. Again, this repentance is post-crucifixion, and the immediate context is not general sin, albeit that idea should not be eliminated from the text, but most appropriately, the repentance conveyed here is that of rejecting Christ.

The crowd's response to Peter's healing of the lame man and his subsequent speech to the temple leaders exceeds the response at Pentecost with Luke's record of five thousand men coming to view Jesus as the Christ.

---

5. Keener, *Acts*, 2:1085.

Peter's Second Address to Temple Rulers (Acts 4:8–12)

Following the previous scene, Peter and John are apprehended by the authorities, who hold them overnight. They are questioned the following day before Annas, Caiaphas, and presumably others who were likely key culprits at Jesus's trial only weeks before. Peter delivers the response, and in doing so, he reiterates the apostolic witness from the first two portions of this study while adding new, unique features. At this point, the expectation is that most, if not all, of this smaller group of elitists are hearing this apostolic presentation synthesizing the news about Jesus for the first time.

Peter follows the pattern of his previous testimony. He connects the healing of the lame man to the person and activity of Jesus, and in describing Jesus, Peter directly states that he was crucified. He is careful to assign blame to the "rulers and elders,"[6] and then he affirms the resurrection of Jesus. Peter then quotes from the Psalms, injecting a new portion of those writings into the Jesus story by quoting, "the stone that was rejected by you, the builders, . . . has become the cornerstone."[7] For the stone to be transformed from rejection to the cornerstone means that its function is no longer rejected but is serving as a vital, principal part of the construct. Moreover, Peter acknowledges the ongoing power associated with Jesus's name by asserting that not only does the lame man's healing derive from that name's ongoing power, but also that "salvation" is related to Jesus's name. Although Peter does not mention the ascension here, this reality is recognized from the content. While this speech is shorter in quantity, Peter provides ample information for his audience to receive an evangelistic presentation.

Peter is filled with the Holy Spirit (Acts 4:8) empowering his speech in a stirring way to these temple rulers (4:13), such that their concern becomes that this healing episode, along with adjacent apostolic speeches, will be enough to further unsettle Jerusalem's inhabitants. Therefore, Peter and John are then ordered to discontinue preaching (4:17). Upon their release, Peter and John return to the apostolic group and reflect upon the fulfillment of Scripture, recognizing that their proclamation is threatening to the various forms of established rule (4:25–28). They, in turn, pray for continued courage as witnesses (4:29–30). As with Peter's Pentecost sermon, a subsequent refrain ends the chapter describing the posture of the

---

6. Acts 4:8.
7. Acts 4:11; see Ps 118:22.

early believers (4:31–37). Within this temple scene, the gospel has been clearly presented, focused on Jesus's death, resurrection, and the current hope provided by the opportunity to believe in Jesus, without the mention of afterlife in any form. Once more, through the message presented here, the early church grows numerically.

Peter's Third Address to the Temple (Acts 5:29–32)

Following Peter and John's interaction with the temple elite in the previous section, they once more return to the temple area and engage the crowds with signs and teaching. This again solicits the attention of temple leaders, who once more question Peter and his companions, now regarding the chief priest's command not to discuss Jesus any further.

Peter's response first affirms his loyalty to God, to the extent of disobeying the chief priest's command. Secondly, Peter provides further Christological dialogue that reinforces Jesus's crucifixion, resurrection, and his ascension, being "exalted" to the "right hand" of God (Acts 5:31). Peter submits that from his new standing, Jesus is offering "repentance to Israel and forgiveness of sins" (5:31). Herein, Peter supplies additional information, conveying Jesus as an able forgiver, clearly because he is again alive and is stationed in proximity to God. Moreover, and again, repentance carries the idea of a needed reversal of their rejection of Jesus, and the forgiveness of sins indicates a pardon for that rejection. However, a new element is introduced, that of forgiveness of sins for Israel. To some degree, this mirrors the words and actions of John the Baptist as he offered a baptism for repentance; however, now Jesus, the one John proclaimed to be greater than he, can offer forgiveness accompanied by Spirit baptism (Luke 3:1–10).[8]

Once more, this third temple address omits elements typically found in contemporary evangelistic approaches. It does not include any mention of an afterlife, except that of Jesus, nor of a relationship of persons to heaven or hell. Repentance is indicated as a necessity of corporate importance for Israel, the covenant-bearers of God. As with his Pentecost speech, Peter concludes by referring to the availability of the Spirit, given by God.

---

8. While space does not permit an exhaustive consideration of this matter, it is worth mentioning that Wright expresses that the forgiveness of sins is synonymous with the return from exile; and as such, rather than being a personal matter between God and the individual, it is more indicative of the collective implications for the restoration of God's people as a community. See Wright, *Jesus and the Victory of God*, 348.

In response to this third expression of the gospel message, the temple rulers become angered and seek to kill Peter and the apostles before being advised otherwise by Gamaliel, who, in a prophetic tone, offers the reasoning that if the movement is of God, then it is unstoppable; and if, on the other hand, it stands against God, then it is unsalvageable, and the apostolic witness will ultimately fail.[9] As a result, the rulers choose to have the apostles beaten rather than executed; however, their punishment fails to deter their public preaching.

Stephen's Speech (Acts 7:1–60)

Just before the narrative flow of Acts moves away from Jerusalem, the reader encounters the lengthiest speech of Luke's writings, delivered by Stephen. Stephen is first introduced as a deacon (6:5) who helps with the distribution of food to widows before becoming a witness himself within a certain synagogue. His precise message within that location is unknown except that his accusers indict him for blasphemy, notably for speaking against Moses, the temple, and the law. As with Peter's second and third speeches, Stephen makes his remarks before the high priest. He summarizes Jewish theological history, remarks on the call of Abraham, discusses the development of circumcision, and describes the relocation of Jacob's family to Egypt, including the later transport of Jacob's bones from Egypt to the promised land (7:2–17). He then narrates the rise and rejection of Moses by his own people before leading them to Sinai for covenant (7:17–36).

The next portion of the speech appears to transition from the telling of Jewish history to more of a Christological commentary, wherein Stephen affirms Moses's words that a prophet would be raised like him (7:37–38). However, Stephen uses the people's rejection of Moses in favor of the golden calf as a parallel to introduce the rejection of Jesus, possibly

---

9. Interestingly, Luke's temple theology is quite extensive, both the captivation with the Jerusalem locale as well as with the eschatological temple. Throughout the Lukan corpus, the temple is a place associated with negative personalities, events, and implications. The lesser and perhaps unexplored aspect of Gamaliel's remark could also be subtly directed toward the temple—that as an operative, if blessed by God, it will withstand any obstacle; however, if positioned in contrast to God, then it will be unsalvageable. Obviously, from historical record, as well as the intentions of Jesus as presented by Luke, the temple is on a trajectory toward demolishment during the period that Luke portrays. An earlier dating of Luke-Acts would suggest those temple events are in close proximity either soon before or after these writings.

prompting the previous accusation of speaking against Moses by comparing him to Jesus (7:37–41). Throughout the speech, Stephen affirms the God of mobility, who journeys with his covenant-bearers through Abram's relocation, Jacob's resettlement in Egypt, and the exodus of the family toward the land of hope, wherein God's presence became personified via the tabernacle (7:44–47). The accusation by his opponents of blaspheming the temple may be indicated when Stephen remarks on Solomon's construct of the temple while inserting the Isaianic text declaring God to be uncontained by human edifices (7:47–50).

At this point, Stephen moves from history and Christology into application by making a rebuttal of his accusers. He goes on the offensive, rebuking them for uncircumcision of ears and hearts as indicated by their resistance to the Holy Spirit (7:51–53). In a culmination of the Jewish story, their rejection of Jesus was part of the lineage of Israel's ongoing record of rejection toward God's prophets and servants, which rendered them murderers and lawbreakers. Just before the crowd drives Stephen outside the town to stone him, he attests to seeing Jesus, the Son of Man, "standing at the right hand of God" (7:54–60).

While the content of Stephen's speech is unique, and in some ways apologetic in nature, it remains functional as an evangelistic presentation. His content shares features in common with Peter's speeches. First, by rendering a telling of the Hebrew story, Stephen anchors the testimony of Jesus within that contextual paradigm. Secondly, Stephen charges his audience, including the high priest, with the rejection of Jesus unto death, the same rebuke given by Peter with the adjacent command to repent for the forgiveness of sins. Third, while affirming Jesus's death, he also supplies a witness to his resurrection and ascension when affirming him to be on site at the right hand of God.

Each of these three components are shared by the Petrine speeches. The primary deviation is that Stephen does not offer the opportunity for repentance and forgiveness to his audience, although that opportunity can perhaps be assumed in the context of his charges to the opponents. However, as literary direction of Acts then shifts to the widespread persecution of the church, the focus is removed from Jerusalem. Since Jerusalem's rejection of Jesus has been the primary cause for the need for repentance and forgiveness, as attested by this study, so, as the narrative flows away from Jerusalem, the record of a call for repentance is omitted. To be clear, it would be an overstatement to suggest that repentance and forgiveness were no longer available to the Jerusalem crowd, but rather, in terms of literary design, the efforts are now exhausted in that location.

Another feature of Stephen's speech worthy of consideration is its subtle introduction to punitive matters regarding potential afterlife. Stephen's final remark is a request for God to release those who stone him from the guilt of their sin. He seeks to eradicate any punitive consequences that might be enacted upon them, perhaps on his behalf, or most likely, for rejecting his message of the gospel. While the potential danger is uncertain, the reference merits brief attention. Moreover, Stephen's prayer is for the "Lord Jesus" to receive his spirit. While this also remains undeveloped, it still hints at the eternality of his person, even though this invocation is distinct from specific gospel transmissions within the text.

Reflecting on the Gospel Transmission in Jerusalem

Thus far, this chapter has considered the Petrine speeches and Stephen's speech, and these narratives provide ample material demonstrating the method of gospel communication in or near Jerusalem, largely to Jewish audiences. Recognizing that Luke's writing could make a distinction between the gospel as delivered to different audiences and locations, it is relevant to synthesize the findings so far.

Two elements are worth noting. First, each transmission of the Jesus story is rooted within Jewish scriptural tradition, wherein Jesus is regarded as the fulfillment and culmination of that story. There is no consistent or isolated approach of telling that story within these speeches; rather, a variety of Old Testament texts are employed. Nevertheless, that commonality is present. It is worth considering that such an approach would naturally connect with the Jewish audience in Jerusalem, as it appeals to a background with which they are quite familiar.

Second, three key structural dynamics used to convey the critical events of his life are Jesus's death, the witness of his resurrection, and the affirmed ascension. In Jerusalem, the preaching identifies the culprits of Jesus's death to be the Jewish audience or their representatives due to their rejection of Jesus. This provides the most direct attestation of sin within the context of the gospel message. However, an embrace of Jesus results in a forgiveness from that sin, and presumably other sins.

These four preaching sessions consistently make no mention of hell, and only slight references to heaven as a place where Jesus resides at the right hand of God. The preaching indicates that the purpose of the Christ event is for a time of refreshing and restoration to arrive, while a rejection of Jesus may lead to negative undefined punitive results.

Both the nature of restoration and judgment are left vague; however, the language regarding restoration is highly correlated to Jewish ideologies of the eschaton when it was believed that Israel would be renewed in a variety of religious, socio-political, and economic ways. However, it appears that the church views itself as already living out the eschaton in Jerusalem through incorporating a common lifestyle.

Diaspora—Moving Outward from Jerusalem

Following the stoning of Stephen, Saul of Tarsus spearheaded the persecution of early believers, resulting in many parties departing Jerusalem. This exit from the holy city enabled the church members to begin to fulfill Jesus's words that they would be witnesses "to the ends of the earth" (Acts 8:1). This section will examine how the good news is announced through Phillip's ministry, Saul's conversion, and Peter's witness to Cornelius.

The Samaritans' Conversion (Acts 8)

Phillip receives the spotlight of the critical scenes in Acts 8. First, he travels to Samaria, where he delivers the gospel. Luke does not convey details of Philip's message, except to say he was "proclaiming Christ" (Acts 8:6) and the "good news about the kingdom of God and the name of Jesus Christ" (8:12). A variety of signs accompanied Philip's message (8:7). Without any additional information of Philip's exact words, it is safe to assume his message about Jesus was in line with that of Peter and Stephen—specifically that Jesus was crucified, risen, ascended, and now offers creation a chance at restoration.

One reason why Luke may have omitted giving details of Philip's testimony relates to the fact that Samaritan beliefs were similar to Jewish tenets. Except for guilt over Jesus's death, Philip would have likely focused his message on pertinent aspects of Torah, including the connection to Moses, because although the Samaritans did not endorse to full Jewish volumes of historical and prophetic writings, they did consider themselves to be the true keepers of Torah. Therefore, it would make sense for them to receive a comparable message to that given in Jerusalem, making it unnecessary for Luke to record the message in detail.

The "Kingdom of God" (Acts 8)

Philip's message does include a unique inclusion in that it references the "kingdom of God," which had not yet been included in any speech thus far in Acts. Jesus had preached of this kingdom both before crucifixion and following resurrection; however, it had not been part of the material conveyed by Luke in Peter's and Stephen's speeches in Jerusalem.

Why was the kingdom not mentioned in the gospel witness in Jerusalem? It could have been because Jesus had already been preaching it in his Galilean ministry, as well as in Judea. Another consideration is that the historical setting made the kingdom-language risky within the Jerusalem political sphere. However, given Luke's theology of God's providence and apostolic assertion, one can hardly conclude that this group would have been too afraid to preach it there. Additionally, political messages were apparently preached in other sensitive Roman locations in Acts, thus largely eliminating that possibility. It could be the message of kingdom was inferred with the language used, including the ascension to God's right hand; however, that would not fully explain the early omission in Jerusalem and later inclusion when delivered to the Samaritans.

A more intriguing consideration is that the juxtaposition of the kingdom message's exclusion in Jerusalem and inclusion in Samaria is deliberate. This would support the idea that the kingdom of God, something that most Jews thought was a concept uniquely reserved for Israel, did not come as expected in the location of Jerusalem, but instead pointedly extends to foreign space beyond those boundaries. The kingdom message's absence in Jerusalem likely points out the rejection of Jesus there, juxtaposed with its declaration in Samaria, where its inclusion was a symbol of the Samaritans' acceptance of the gospel. Regardless, the reason Luke injects the language when addressing Samaria is subordinate to the central focus of the narrative, which is the expression of their tremendous reception of the good news.

CHAPTER 12: THE GOSPEL MESSAGE OF ACTS

The Ethiopian Eunuch's Kingdom Encounter (Acts 8:26–40)

Philip's message is next relayed to the Ethiopian eunuch, who, like the Samaritans, represents a nuanced category of people. This man is reading the Isaiah scroll, so therefore, although he is Ethiopian, he appears to already have an interest in Judaism. In the intentional trajectory of Acts, the good news is preached first to Jews in Jerusalem; secondly, presented by Stephen, a Hellenistic Jew in proximity to Jerusalem; and third, by Philip to half-Jews in Samaria. It is logical to conclude that this Ethiopian represents the next progressive category, that being a gentile convert to Judaism. The author includes fewer remarks regarding Philip's message to this man than in the previous scene; however, the apostolic approach is consistent, telling the Jesus story in cooperation with Hebrew tradition.

Plainly, the Isaianic passage, the subject of the Ethiopian's reading, is used in Acts with Christological interpretation. The progression at this point demonstrates an extensive volume of words supplied to the Jerusalem crowds, yet these are met with rejection by the leaders; then fewer words are rendered to the Samaritans, yet they are receptive. Finally, in this instance, Luke hardly records any remarks to the Ethiopian, yet with this small effort, he affirms Jesus. Luke's authorial method is to show through the narrative flow that, as the gospel drifts further from Jerusalem geographically, ethnically, and ideologically, fewer words are necessary to record, perhaps indicating the more open reception to Jesus that is ready and waiting outside of Jerusalem.

Saul's Damascus Road Encounter (Acts 9:1–31)

The next scene moves to describe the event with Saul of Tarsus. Scholarship has debated whether the events associated with his Damascus Road experience represent a calling or conversion. Nevertheless, this study acknowledges that, at this time, the Jesus story was revealed to Saul in sufficient measure to count as gospel transmission. Saul is blinded as he travels to Damascus to persecute Christians, and while variances to this account are recorded in Acts, the consistent detail is that he heard the voice of Jesus give a clear indication of resurrection and perhaps even the ascension.

This testimony from Jesus in Saul's encounter quite obviously changes his life trajectory and causes him to believe the message. In the adjacent scene, Ananias is informed that Saul will take the name of the Lord to

"Gentiles and kings and the people of Israel" (Acts 9:15). Upon Ananias's arrival to meet Saul, the latter receives the filling of the Holy Spirit, which for Luke always accompanies speech. Saul was then baptized in water. The text states that Saul "immediately" began to preach Jesus, referring to him as the "Son of God" (9:20). This is the initial time in the Lukan corpus that a human witness has affirmed Jesus with such a characterization, a description which also carries a Davidic connotation (Acts 13:33). This significantly correlates with the doctrine of resurrection and ascension, two principal elements of gospel presentation in Acts, and secures the Jesus story within the framework of Hebrew tradition.

Cornelius's Kingdom Encounter (Acts 10:1–48)

The next key event in Acts is Peter preaching in Caesarea to Cornelius, a gentile but also a "God-fearing man" (Acts 10:2). Here again is a character in Acts who represents a category of individuals who maintain respect for Torah but who have not converted to Judaism outright. Luke supplies a lengthy narrative, first detailing the events leading to Peter gaining comfort with the occasion, then the reception of Cornelius and his household, followed by Peter's apologetic of the events in Jerusalem. Part of the message is that "what God has made clean you must not consider ritually unclean" (10:15). The implication is the gospel transcends traditional Jewish categories, in part physically demonstrated by Peter entering the home of Cornelius (10:28), who would have been perceived as an unclean gentile.

Peter's message to Cornelius presents a radical experience which is predicated on a vision given to Peter that reformulated traditional viewpoints. This message is distinct from that given to the Ethiopian eunuch, who happened to be traveling with Scripture in hand, waiting for an interpreter for the gospel implications in Isaiah. Providence unmistakably places Peter and Cornelius together, and Peter's proclamation includes remarks on the eradication of ethnic and nationalistic favoritism (10:34) and favor being transplanted to those who walk justly (10:35).

Jesus is the "good news of peace" to Israel, hence fulfilling the Israel story (10:36). It is told this way: Jesus went through Galilee establishing his works of power, including resisting the devil (10:38); however, in Jerusalem, the hearers rejected Jesus and crucified him (10:39), but he arose from the dead (10:40). Two additional key features include a matter of judgment, wherein Peter asserts that Jesus is "appointed by God as judge of the living

CHAPTER 12: THE GOSPEL MESSAGE OF ACTS

and dead" (10:42). This active role infers the doctrine of ascension. While judgment is a relevant factor, the word denotes the highest reigning authority, which is consistent with ascension theology, and does not solely or primarily indicate punitive matters. The matters of afterlife and heaven or hell are not directly described in this chapter, and while judgment of living and dead are mentioned, it is a mistake to overstate these elements into a formed view of afterlife including heaven and hell as potential components given the absence of this material in Acts.

Moreover, Peter affirms Jesus as the continuation of the Hebrew story by attesting that "all the prophets testify" about Jesus that "everyone who believes in him receives forgiveness of sins through his name" (10:43). However, this concept for belief far exceeds intellectual agreement, instead conferring a sense of loyalty and devotion.[10]

Beyond the statement that forgiveness of sins is received, to whose sins does Peter refer when he addresses Cornelius? The more commonly held perception is that Peter references the general sins of all humanity, and this is certainly possibly if not likely. However, nowhere is Cornelius told to repent of any sins. Alternatively, Peter could be discussing the sins in the same context he previously employed, as sins that occurred in Jerusalem. This would represent logical consistency in the vein of the Hebrew story as Jesus is presented. Of course, the events in Jerusalem are also associated with the Roman authority which carried out Jesus's execution; therefore, Rome was not exempt of this guilt either, which is perhaps inferred upon the centurion.

At this point, it is preliminary to make any conclusive assertions about the exact meaning of "sins" in this statement. The importance of the occasion is the Holy Spirit's arrival upon Cornelius and other listeners, and that Peter in turn baptizes them. Its significance is reemphasized as the event is relayed over again in a mirror account in Jerusalem in the following chapter, as Peter presents a defense for the Holy Spirit being distributed and the gospel being extended to a Roman gentile household.

The Pauline Witness

Acts 13:1–3 marks a formal commissioning of Saul, who is thereafter referred to by his Greek name Paul. He is sent throughout the Mediterranean world preaching both in Jewish synagogues and among the broader gentile

---

10. See Bates, *Gospel Allegiance*; see also Bates, *Salvation by Allegiance*.

populace. This section will follow the gospel message in the Pauline mission to Jews and gentiles throughout the Mediterranean world.

Paul's Message of the Good News in Antioch

In Acts 13:16–42, Paul appeals to Jews and God-fearing gentiles at Antioch through a lengthy speech in a synagogue. It is likely that most in this audience had not previously received a thorough record of the Jesus witness, if any record at all. Paul sets the stage by telling a tale of Jewish history, from the time of slavery in Egypt through the forty years in the wilderness, the settlement in their land, the period of judges, the time of Samuel, and eventually the time of Saul, the first anointed king. This primes the story for the introduction of David, offered as an ideal king, and to declare that through his descendant, Jesus, the promises of God are now available. Paul makes note of John the Baptist but emphasizes the superiority of Jesus before proclaiming the arrival of God's salvation. He then proceeds to assert Jesus's rejection by the Jerusalem rulers. This resulted in Jesus's death that led to resurrection and confirmation of Sonship, which in turn indicates ascension.

The benefit of this reality, as Paul states, is that the listeners are now justified in belief in a way wherein the Mosaic law was unable to justify them, such that the forgiveness of sins has been offered. From the Lukan perspective, even as new information is introduced concerning justification, this remark that is lightly used in Lukan theology should not be made into a comprehensive doctrine. If sin is principally considered from the aspect of Messianic rejection, then it seems congruent that the Mosaic law has no provision for such a pardon. Therefore, the justification as offered by Jesus, with the opportunities associated with his resurrection, is that he might extend forgiveness, permitting a potential for repentance, which would have otherwise been impossible.

However, many of those in the synagogue reject this message. This leads Paul toward a ministry directed to gentiles, fulfilling a prophetic missiological perspective in bringing "salvation to the ends of the earth" (Acts 1:8). Once more, a major anchor to the gospel presentation is the fulfillment of Jewish history, in that Jesus is seen as compensating for possible limitations of Mosaic law, wherein he was rejected, crucified, and has risen with theological implications concerning his ongoing activity, all of which serve to direct attention toward his elevation into ascension.

CHAPTER 12: THE GOSPEL MESSAGE OF ACTS

Herein, from a contemporary Western evangelical perspective, the absence of the mention of heaven and hell is notable in this section, and the only regard for afterlife is the reference to Jesus fulfilling the psalmist's affirmation. Additionally, modern perspectives regarding justification are distinct from ancient understandings. The Lukan presentation of the gospel is not delivered in the post-Reformation era when debates over justification concerned its juxtaposition with or opposition to Mosaic law. Paul's voice does not demean the law, but remarks on its limitations given Israel's great sin of Messianic rejection. The Lukan record in Acts presents the early church as deeply concerned with the law, even to the point of compliance with many standards, while negotiating its applications elsewhere. However, in Lukan theology, the loyalty of Christ supplies justification that exceeds the limits of the law but does not absolutely supplant it.

The Gospel in Iconium and Lystra (Acts 14:1–20)

Acts 14 records that at Iconium, as Paul and Barnabas minister in the Jewish synagogue to both Jews and Greeks, "the Lord . . . testified to the message of his grace" (14:3) which is the initial time that grace is directly attributed to the gospel messages recorded in Acts.

This concept of grace is not that which was defined in the post-Reformation setting of the West, as a philosophical contemplation of unmerited favor; this is grace according to a first-century understanding in a world where it functioned as a gift mechanism that would engage the recipient in a reciprocal relationship. If there is any sense within the Lukan context of salvation or the good news being about relationship, it would be in this context of reciprocity, where one party extends grace, and the receiver then returns it after a different manner.[11]

In Lystra, in the adjacent scene in the same chapter, Paul and Barnabas characterize the gospel as people turning from pagan gods and their sacrifices and fixating upon the God of creation who blesses them. They are not told to repent of sin or threatened with punishment; however, conceptually, repentance from idolatrous gods is inferred.

---

11. See Barclay, *Paul and the Gift*.

The Gospel in Philippi (Acts 16:11–40)

The early church movement spreads to Philippi, a critical Roman settlement wherein the socio-economic status quo is disrupted by Paul's casting a spirit out of a slave girl. Since this liberates her and causes her to lose her gift of divination, it causes her owners to lose profit, an economic upheaval which leads to Paul and Silas's imprisonment. During this time, their prayers and singing are heard by God such that an earthquake opens an escape avenue for the detainees. This offers the chance to share the gospel message, as the jailer who is responsible for the prisoners at the expense of his own life prepares to commit suicide; yet, Paul stays his hand, alerting him that the prisoners have remained voluntarily. The jailer's response in 16:30 echoes that of the Jews in Acts 2:37: "Sirs, what must I do to be saved?"

The word *saved* takes on various contexts within the world of Scripture. Even within Luke's writings, it is used in different ways. What is this jailer asking to be saved from? The book of Acts makes no mention of hell. Meanwhile, the concept of judgment has been presented only lightly, especially outside of Jerusalem. Perhaps the jailer inquires how he might be saved from self-harm, or from vulnerability to execution. While this jailer's specific motivation and intentions are unknown, the apostles distinctly direct him, "believe in the Lord Jesus and you will be saved."

At this point, given the track record of gospel presentation, it is reasonable to conclude that this "belief" in Jesus implies an affirmation of matters discussed previously—namely, the fulfillment of Jewish history in the life of Jesus, his rejection, crucifixion, resurrection, and active role in ascension offering restoration and authority. Moreover, since the jailer had been close to taking his life, it would be expected that the apostles initially shared the most abbreviated form of gospel presentation, which would have later been supplemented with these further instructional qualities. After all, the man is noted to be baptized that very night, a strange occurrence indeed, and this would have been unlikely had Paul not first provided a more thorough demonstration of the Jesus message. Therefore, the understanding in the text is that this conversion and baptism followed reception of a gospel message that aligned with previous testimony.

CHAPTER 12: THE GOSPEL MESSAGE OF ACTS

The Gospel in Thessalonica and Berea (Acts 17:1–15)

Paul and Silas reach Thessalonica where they proclaim Christ in his sufferings and resurrection. While the extent of their message beyond that description is unknown, it is remarkable that what they share provokes those who resist Paul to make a political accusation against him akin to treason (17:7). Paul's gospel to the Thessalonians, in addition to other places, necessarily conveys a political connotation. The "good news" proclaims that Jesus is to be referred to as the Son of God and that he is ruling, seated at the right hand of God. At Berea, Luke notes that the synagogue attendees searched the Scripture to confirm Paul's message, consistent with the evidence that the Jesus message is to be viewed as the continuation and fulfillment of the Hebrew story and scriptures.

The Gospel in Athens (Acts 17:16–34)

A key scene in Acts is Paul's engagement at Athens, a cultural and intellectual seat known for various philosophies. The Athenians acknowledge that Paul speaks "the good news about Jesus and the resurrection" (17:18). As attested in the witness thus far, one cannot speak about Jesus's resurrection without his crucifixion. Additionally, the ascension is what is always directly mentioned or inferred in the material in connection with Jesus's ongoing Christological vocation.

As Paul is given opportunity to develop his presentation more thoroughly before the Athenian group, he appeals to their acknowledgment of ignorance, referencing "an unknown God." Paul's assertion is that God is not made by human hands (idols) nor contained by human constructs (temples), but is the author and sustainer of all life, and now demands repentance of all people. Herein is one of the few examples where repentance is mentioned to a gentile audience. The context occurs with clarity, that this repentance indicates a turn from pagan idolatry toward a recognition of the "unknown god" that Paul affirms as creator. Finally, Paul mentions judgment, inferring afterlife and sin, but without remarking on heaven or hell. The purpose of these remarks by Paul is to attest the present activity of Jesus as the judge of the world.

Paul's Message from Jerusalem to Rome (Acts 21:1—28:31)

Paul's travel to Jerusalem and his subsequent detention and relocation to Rome provide multiple instances that impart brief but useful contributions to the gospel presentation. First, as Paul was giving an account of his own gospel reception, he adds material concerning Ananias, who was told that Paul was chosen by "the God of our ancestors." The narrative further declares that Paul would see and hear the "Righteous One," as in the resurrected Lord (22:14), and that Paul was baptized, having his sins washed away (22:16). These sins are likely associated with Paul's persecution of the church. Each these details delivers further affirmation of the good news as the continuation of Jewish history.

In front of the Sadducees and Pharisees, Paul prompts a debate by pinning the entire issue on the matter of resurrection, a distinct hallmark of gospel presentation (23:6). Moreover, if on some level the gospel must be reduced to a single word, it would be resurrection, on which both the crucifixion and ascension hinge.

As the story continues, Luke continues to include details linking the good news with its Jewish past. In Acts 24, when Paul is giving testimony, he affirms the worship of the "God of our ancestors" (24:14), connecting himself to the law and prophets as well as to Israel's history (24:14). Moreover, he affirms his hope in the resurrection, which for the first time in the Lukan corpus is directly linked to a human; however, this includes both the righteous and unrighteous (24:15). Paul indicates that the resurrection leads to judgment and that this is the reason why he maintains a clear conscience (24:16).

Later, within the same chapter, Paul again gives an affirmation about judgment to Felix (24:25). Paul again testifies of the promises of God made to the Israel story, that are fulfilled in the resurrection (26:8). Meanwhile he conveys the story of his conversion a second time (the third time total in Acts), describing the voice of Christ witnessing to him and telling him that his vocation would be toward the gentiles, who are able to receive forgiveness of sins (26:18).

The context of forgiveness becomes more pertinent at this portion of Acts, and it seems based on the context of Acts, as well as verse 18, that the people's need for forgiveness is for their ignorance regarding idolatry, which was pervasive in antiquity, and for their surrender to the powers of Satan. Paul also provides information regarding the repentance preached in Jerusalem, which is associated with turning to God (26:20) rather than referring to general sins. The context is that this is needed because of the rejection of Jesus, as discussed previously. In the final portion of Paul's testimony, he affirms Jesus as the fulfillment of prophets and Moses (26:22) through his sufferings and resurrection (26:23).

In the concluding chapter of Acts, Paul, in Rome, testifies of the "kingdom of God" based on Mosaic law and prophets, again as the continuation of Jewish history (28:23). Curiously, the "kingdom of God" phrasing has been largely absent in Acts, but here it reappears, at the conclusion, in Rome of all places. In addition, the concluding verse of the corpus (28:31) proclaims Paul as preaching this kingdom of God and about the Lord Jesus Christ with "boldness," adding an intriguing dynamic within the Roman context.

A Synthesis of Gospel Proclamation in Acts

Having surveyed the gospel presentation in Acts, this chapter will now briefly overview the use of key concepts related to evangelism. These include the book of Acts' use of the phrases "good news" or gospel; "salvation"; "sins" and "forgiveness"; and finally, "repentance" and "grace."

The "Good News"

The Greek εὐαγγέλιον (*euaggelion*, "good news") and εὐαγγελίζω (*euaggelizó*, "proclaiming the good news") are the principal words this study identifies as denoting "gospel." Luke's Gospel uses this expression in varied ways, with this section examining these words and immediate cognates. Gabriel tells Zechariah the "good news" of the forthcoming birth of John the Baptist (1:19), the initial Gospel occurrence, and Luke's first volume often associates these words with the societally, economically, or physically impoverished, and the unveiling of God's salvation plan. In Acts, the words for "gospel" appear seventeen times; however, in the context of Jerusalem or broader Jewish Palestine, it is only used once, and that time in a generic (non-specific) form (Acts 5:22).

The remaining sixteen instances of the "gospel" in Acts appear in the context of the message spreading outward. The expression is used twice to the Samaritans (8:4, 12), three times in connection with the Ethiopian eunuch (8:25, 35, 40), once with relation to Cornelius (10:36), and five times regarding the church in Antioch (11:20; 13:22; 14:7, 15, 21). In each of those eleven cases, it is used in gentile contexts. Then, although the expression "gospel" is used at the Jerusalem Council in Acts 15:7, the context is gentile inclusion. After that, it is used once more at Antioch (15:35). Subsequently, in Acts 16, Paul has a vision to cross into Macedonia, marking a critical geographic transition in the narrative, at which point the narrative remarks on the "gospel" in the gentile region (16:10) as well as in Athens (17:18). Finally, in Acts 20:24, Paul gives a summary of his life's activity, describing the gospel as his priority. The unique attestation regarding the words for "gospel" used in Acts is that, with only one exception, it always occurs within gentile contexts.

Salvation

The next critical words to consider are σῴζω (*sózó*, "saved") and σωτηρία (*sótéria*, "salvation"). In the Gospel, Luke uses these words and close derivatives connected to a variety of matters ranging from personal healings to broader salvation and eschatological matters. In Acts, it is first used in Jerusalem at Pentecost in relationship to Peter's preaching and a positive Jewish response (2:21, 40, 47). It occurs in Jerusalem (4:9, 12) when Peter preaches following the healing of a lame man, and when Stephen discusses Jewish history (7:25). Peter then uses the term concerning Cornelius (11:14).

During the Pauline ministry, "salvation" is used in a variety of ways. It is included within the Jewish story (13:26) but is later given to the gentiles (13:47). It is used as the basis for the Jerusalem Council (15:1) and as the affirmation of gentile salvation (15:11). In Philippi, the oracles of divination within the slave girl declare that Paul and his companions are "proclaiming . . . the way of salvation" in (16:17), and afterward, the jailer inquiries about this salvation (16:30–31). Finally, it is used three times in chapter 20 (20:20, 31, 34) during Paul's voyage to Rome regarding the travelers' safety from the storm.

Naturally, the question posed is the nature of salvation. From what do people need rescuing or saving? Acts does not precisely delimit this answer. As with "gospel," in the broader Roman context, the idea of "salvation" was often used to refer to a political plan to bring stability to the world.[12] While salvation in Acts clearly includes sins, it should not be narrowed down to only that association; nor does the word strictly apply to judgment, or hell, the latter of which fails to appear in Acts at all. Most

---

12. Borg and Crossan, *First Christmas*, 159.

likely, the word should be used holistically as indicative of the broader creation, which prominently includes humans, but encompassing the new heavens and earth—an idea shared and likely borrowed from the Roman political usage of the same terms.[13]

Sins/Forgiveness

The Greek word ἁμαρτία (*hamartia*, "a sin, a failure") and its near relatives are used for the word for "sin." It is used generically in Luke's Gospel (in most cases, without specific examples of the types of sin). In Acts, it is referenced eight times. In three instances (Acts 2:38, 3:19, and 5:31), the word is directed toward Jerusalem audiences, when the predominant concern is the misdeed of rejecting Jesus. It is again employed at a Jerusalem audience in Stephen's prayer for God not to hold his accusers' sins against them (7:60), an obvious attestation of Christological rejection displayed via the stoning of Stephen. In Acts 22:16, Paul's testimony connects sins to baptism that washes them away. Again, this is used with a Jewish audience, and most directly addresses the Messianic rejection. The other two instances of the word "sin" in Acts to Jewish audiences also reference to gentile inclusion, first when Paul is at a synagogue (13:38), and then before the Jewish authorities (26:18). The most direct reference of sins to a gentile is with Peter's preaching to Cornelius (Acts 10:43) where he attests the prophetical lineage speaks to the forgiveness of sins extending from Jesus.

The words ἄφεσις (*aphesis*, "dismissal, release, pardon") and ἀφίημι (*aphiémi*, "to send away, leave alone, permit") both pertain to forgiveness with their close cognates and are used in an applicable context in Acts five times. Acts 2:38 and 5:31 are directed toward Israel for the forgiveness for sins in the context of rejecting Jesus. When Peter is preaching to Cornelius, telling him the story of Jesus, he remarks on the forgiveness associated with Christ (10:43). At a synagogue, among Jewish recipients, Paul remarks on forgiveness being offered through Christ (13:38). Upon speaking to Jewish authorities, Paul remarks on forgiveness to Jews and gentiles (26:18). Therefore, except for the story of Cornelius, when sins and forgiveness are mentioned in Acts, they are used in presentations to Jewish audiences.

---

13. Borg and Crossan, *First Christmas*, 154.

Repentance/Grace/Faith

The words μετανοέω (*metanoeó*, "repent") and μετάνοια (*metanoia*, "change of mind, repentance") appear in Acts in theological content eight times.[14] In Jerusalem, it is associated with reversing the Jewish rejection of Jesus (2:38, 3:19, 5:31). Next, again among Jews at the Jerusalem, the crowd gives thanks that repentance is offered to the gentiles (11:18). In Athens, Paul uses it (17:34) when speaking to the Athenians about repenting, turning from the gods of idolatry and turning toward the God of Abraham. Acts 20:21 describes Paul as telling both Jews and gentiles about repentance; and later, when testifying to Jewish authorities, Paul speaks of his own calling toward the gentiles—that they can repent and do the works associated with repentance (26:20).

Also, in Acts, χάρις (*charis*, "grace") and its immediate derivatives appear seventeen times. However, the words have broad associations with favorable views and actions within social relationships, at times beyond theological conceptions; therefore, this section delimits itself to those that are applicable.[15] In Jerusalem, grace is only mentioned in terms of being active within the church and among its servants (2:47, 4:33, 6:8); however, as the message starts to quickly spread to the broader regions that include predominantly gentile areas, the word is used in association to these areas coming to faith (11:23; 13:43; 14:3, 26; 18:27). Grace is used with a direct soteriological meaning at the Jerusalem Council when, through the grace of Jesus, both Jew and gentile are attested to find salvation. In Acts 20:24 and 32, when Paul is making his way back to Jerusalem, he considers his testimony as being of God's grace. In all these cases, the word, in its most fundamental aspect, is not used by Luke as describing God's generosity to allow an escape from hell; and it is not used as a rhetorical strategy to produce faith. In fact, the word *grace* is not used in any of the speeches that convey the gospel proclamation, although God's grace is apparent. Rather, grace functions as a mechanism for extending favor, and as a means of initiating relationships.

---

14. There are other instances where these words appear denoting material inapplicable to this study, referring to other cognitive or geographical changes disassociated with any theological application.

15. See Malina, "Grace/Favor."

CHAPTER 12: THE GOSPEL MESSAGE OF ACTS

Reflecting on the Gospel Message of the Early Church

Based on the evidence of the book of Acts, sharing the Jesus witness includes distinct critical elements. First, Jesus is the continuation and fulfillment of Israel's story, and the prophets and broader corpus of Hebrew scriptures evidenced his arrival. Second, Jesus lived and demonstrated his uniqueness through a series of public signs and actions. Third, the Jewish authorities, in collusion with the Romans, arrested Jesus, placed him on trial, and crucified him. Fourth, Jesus rose from the dead and ascended to God's right hand. This is the Jesus story and the culmination of Israel's history.

The good news is realized in the message that Jesus is now alive and reigns as Lord and Christ. In his current state, Jesus offers the forgiveness of sins, which includes a twofold function as it is applied to the immediate sin of messianic rejection and secondly to general sins of neglect or ignorance. The grace, or favor, of Christ is displayed in the opportunity for forgiveness, but also in the chance to be in alignment with his rule.

The message demands certain responses. What is required of humanity is a repentance, a turning away from the rejection of Jesus, or from substitutes for Jesus (idols) for those who have never heard the message. In addition, the message requires listeners to place faith (loyalty, fidelity) in Jesus, who reigns.

The message also includes the benefits of this faith. The corporate benefits include the opportunity to repair the wrongs of history (now to embrace rather than reject Jesus) and to cooperate with God's design for creation, and a general but non-specific restoration of all things. The personal benefits are that those pledging their faith will be on the right side of judgment (although how that works is uncertain); will receive his forgiveness and grace (relational opportunities); and will personally experience the resurrection potential of all matter.

This survey offers a needful opportunity for further research and application, primarily when compared to popularized movements extending from the post-Reformation, into the Great Awakenings of North America, into the rise of evangelical methods of tracts, crusades, and methodological approaches, and how these contemporary developments might compare and contrast to the gospel presentation in Acts.

Chapter 13: Where's the Love?

An Exploration of the Infrequent Theme in Luke-Acts

Introduction

"GOD LOVES YOU AND has a plan for your life." This is a familiar phrase to many Christians, with some perceiving these words as essential to the gospel presentation. However, it may come as a surprise that within the Lukan corpus, which accounts for roughly 27 percent of the New Testament, and therefore the most substantial portion, the use of the word *love* is largely absent. Love is incorporated into the Pauline and Johannine texts in far greater magnitude than it is in Luke-Acts.[1]

In Acts, with one modest exception, love is missing altogether. That exception occurs in 15:25 when the Jerusalem Council dispatches a letter describing Barnabas and Paul as *agapetos*, with English translations mixed between "beloved" and "dear friends." In any event, this portion is hardly evidential. Luke includes carefully articulated and constructed speeches in Acts, many of which include the early *kerygma*, yet noticeably, no attempt is made to employ the words commonly translated as "love," *agapao* and *phileo*, or their cognates.

These words and their derivatives appear in Luke's Gospel, but never in the context of direct application of God's love for humanity or his broader creation. Readers will not see "God loves you" in this text. Rather, they will see two powerful instances of God's love for his Son; and they will encounter examples of people's love for each other. These latter usages of love tend to occur in the context of the robust Lukan themes of status reversal,

---

1. This chapter is an adaptation of a paper that was read at the 2022 Southeastern Regional Meeting of the Evangelical Theological Society at Bob Jones University, Greenville, South Carolina, on March 25, 2022.

economic and material ethics, and ministry to the marginalized, including women and non-Jews. In recognizing this context, readers gain a picture of what love should look like in the kingdom of God.

The aim of this chapter is to develop Luke's concept of love, both in terms of interpersonal relationships and in terms of God's connection to creation, by considering each instance of the use of love in the gospel and its context. It will also uncover where love may be found in Acts, although indirectly articulated.

Scholarship Gap in Luke-Acts

While its hypothesis is straightforward, the import of this chapter is that the vast magnitude of sources focusing on Luke-Acts have neglected love as an overall theme. While exegetes confront individual aspects of love in the Lukan corpus, rarely is love considered in Luke-Acts as a whole, and then insufficiently. As a contribution beginning to fill this gap in Lukan theology, this article highlights Luke's overall view of love in Luke-Acts.

The lack of scholarly resources devoted to this theme within Luke-Acts is so overwhelming that it creates a challenge when it comes to producing a demonstrable gap in literature. As an example, Darrell Bock's extensive *A Theology of Luke and Acts* offers the most quantitative treatment of Lukan theology. To his credit, Bock is perhaps the only one who does acknowledge love as a theme in Luke. However, it is still somewhat alarming that even in Bock's lengthy work, a space of less than a page is given to the treatment of love. Furthermore, in that section, Bock does not mention Acts at all. Furthermore, although he does draw on four Lukan passages in the discussion of love, strangely, part of the space on this single page is devoted to four texts from non-Lukan epistles. In addition, of the Lukan texts referenced, two do not mention love at all, nor is their primary context or aim regarding love.[2] This makes the actual material covering love in Luke utterly limited in Bock's treatment.

The fact that Bock's work may be the only one to offer a summarizing biblical theology of love in Luke-Acts, and yet it still addresses the topic so

---

2. In the section entitled "Love for God and for One's Neighbor," Bock highlights the Lukan passages of Luke 10:25–37 in what includes the parable of the good Samaritan. He also references Luke 6:27–36, 11:1–13, and 10:38–42. The latter two do not mention love. Furthermore, Bock does not draw from Acts in his presentation of love within Lukan theology. See Bock, *Theology of Luke and Acts*.

sparsely, is exemplary of the overall omission in scholarship regarding love in the Lukan texts. In addition, the marked absence of discussion of this topic in Acts is unusual, as the text is certainly worthy of consideration in a chapter dedicated to discovering the author's theology of love.

God's Love in Luke—Bookends of the Gospel

Having noted the gap in this area of study, this treatment begins with Luke's initial and final deployment of the word *agapao* and its cognate *agapetos* in the Gospel, which come from chapters 3 and 20, respectively. These are the only two occasions in Luke-Acts in which love is directly referenced as being extended from the Father. In both cases, the context is clear. The love being expressed is in relation to Jesus.

"You are my son, whom I love." (Luke 3:22 NIV)

It is pertinent to recognize that when this *agapao* is first articulated toward Jesus, the occasion is his baptism. At that event, the heavens open, the Holy Spirit descends and attaches to Jesus, and then the voice expresses love from the Father toward the Son.

The moment of Jesus's baptism also marks the first direct association between Jesus and the Spirit, a connection which plays a pivotal role in prompting Jesus to enter the wilderness for his testing (4:1–13). The Spirit then compels Jesus back to Galilee, and eventually to Nazareth, within the same chapter (4:14–16). There Jesus reads the Isaianic text in the synagogue, affirming in his message that "the spirit of the Lord is upon me" (4:18–19).

From a social-scientific perspective, Bruce Malina rightly observes that in contrast to modern Western thinking, love within the world of the text was not primarily an emotional attachment, but rather it was a relational quality.[3] This was the result of a collectivistic worldview in which group orientation was essential and identity was formed by the people's dyad, or surrounding components.

The Spirit being given to Jesus is part of the sign and demonstration of the Father's love. It is relational. Both the Holy Spirit and the Father become embedded in Jesus's identity as his Sonship is affirmed at baptism. This is unsurprising considering the pronouncement in Luke 1:35 that the Holy Spirit would be an agent of Jesus's birth. From that point, Sonship is highlighted multiple times. Twelve-year-old Jesus asserts in Luke 2:49 that he must be

---

3. Reese and Pilch, "Love," 106–9.

about his Father's business. In Luke 3:22, the affirmation of Sonship takes place at his baptism. Following this, Jesus defends this status to the tempter (4:1–13) before his Sonship plays a pertinent role in the dispute in Nazareth, where the question is asked, "Is this not Joseph's son?" (4:22).

Through these early progressions, Luke establishes a Sonship relationship that becomes functionally ignited at Jesus's baptism and Holy Spirit reception. With the advent of the Spirit, Jesus's vocation is defined, his motivations are made apparent, and he becomes led by the Spirit, serving in a prophetic and healing ministry and combating unclean spirits. This is the outcome of the Father's relational love for the Son in connection with the Spirit.

> "I will send my son, whom I love." (Luke 20:13 NIV)

The second occurrence that articulates the Father's love toward the Son appears in parabolic form in Luke 20:13. In the parable of the tenants (20:9–19), Jesus relates the words of the owner of the vineyard, who says, "I will send my son, whom I love." It is largely uncontested that the master of the vineyard depicts God, and accordingly, that the son within the parable represents Jesus. The love, or relationship, between a father and son, presumably his heir and firstborn, is undeniable.

As represented in this parable, Jesus's role correlates to the heir of the vineyard. It is also conceivable to analogize this as indicating that Jesus is the heir of God's ultimate creation with the vocation of stewardship. This fits with a Lukan perspective, which aligns sonship not only genealogically through Abraham in the context of Israel, but also historically through descent from the line of Adam, son of God (Luke 3:38), who was also given a divine task in the stewardship of creation.

The two uses of *agapao* at the beginning and end of Luke demonstrate an overlap among the Father's love toward Jesus, the relational connection of sonship, and the bestowal of the Holy Spirit, with particular attention paid at his baptism.

God's Love in Acts—Sonship and Baptism

In Luke-Acts, baptism of water and Spirit are tied to initiation occurrences.[4] Accordingly, as Jesus's ministry is being initiated, the Father, in a most direct way, has attached to Jesus, embedded the Holy Spirit within him, and

---

4. Dunn, "Baptism in Holy Spirit," 7.

articulated his love for him. Additionally, divine vocation intertwines with love and Sonship, not only based on inference from the parable of the tenants, but also evident in Jesus's actions following his baptism.

Given these characteristics in relation to Jesus in Luke, it becomes evident that in Acts, the Father's love can be attested via the Holy Spirit's transmission. The early record of the *ecclesia* in some ways parallels Jesus's experience and actions. The same Spirit that joins with Jesus as evidence and affirmation of the Father's love is then joined to the church following his ascension. As with the account of the Spirit descending like a dove in Luke 3 in connection with Jesus's baptism, Holy Spirit reception is tied to water baptism throughout Acts. Furthermore, like Jesus, at the advent of the Spirit, the church receives a clear vocational mission—first, to be witnesses, and then to live out Jesus's message in the Christ community. The Spirit is depicted as directing the early church, enabling them to conduct miracles and actions mirroring those of Jesus.

While the words translated "love" are absent from Luke's second volume, the parallelism of the love language of Luke 3 is quite evident in Acts via the Holy Spirit's dispersion and attachment to the *ecclesia*. More directly stated, while Acts omits the words translated as "love," the book clearly demonstrates God's love for the church via the Holy Spirit attachment and through the enabling of a variety of gifts. This view of love in Acts is substantiated not only textually, but also through Malina's social-scientific assessment of love as a social attachment.

Positive Relational Love in Luke

Having dealt with the only two Lukan expressions of love emanating from God himself, the remaining instances of love in Luke, which constitute the majority, must be considered. These take place via interpersonal relationships. Luke's uses of the word *love* appear deliberate, occurring in confluence with rich theological themes, and often amid neighboring passages with Lukan-only material.

Positive uses of "love" take place in Luke 6–10, beginning with the Sermon on the Plain and extending through the parable of the good Samaritan, again with an observable parallel in Acts. In contrast, Luke's negative uses of "love" occur in connection with the Pharisees, lawyers, and scribes. Throughout these briefly examined cases, Luke leaves his

CHAPTER 13: WHERE'S THE LOVE?

readers to reflect on the point he is making regarding status reversal and socio-economic ethics in God's kingdom.

Love in Luke 6:20–49—Sermon on the Plain

The Sermon on the Plain provides several instances of love: "*agapao* your enemies, do good to those who hate you" (6:27); "If you *agapao* those who *agapao* you, then where is the credit?" (6:33); and "*agapao* your enemies" (6:35). While this section appears to share the same source as Matthew chapters 5–7, the context is surrounded by rich, Lukan-unique content in his Sermon on the Plain that compares and even contrasts to the Matthean Sermon on the Mount. Herein, Luke asserts status reversal and a sequence of socio-economic ethics. Not only are the blessings on the poor, hungry, weeping, and despised invoked in an affirmation of reversal, but these appear to be expressed at the expense of the of their wealthy, well-fed, and otherwise satisfied counterparts. Furthermore, following a series of blessings as in Matthew, Luke shares the additionally complicated dimensions of love by compelling those who are stricken to turn the cheek, to provide a tunic to those who take their coat, and to give without expectation of return.

In considering this case of interpersonal relationships, it would be reductionistic to limit Luke's presentation to portraying love as a social equalizer; however, the component of rebalancing, particularly in terms of the reversal between the poor and rich, the hungry and well fed, and mourners with the joyful is undeniable and unavoidable. In the concept of this broader sermon, loving one's enemies and giving without the expectation of return indicates the surrender of conventional ethics. Instead of promoting the value of individual preservation and self-assertion, one becomes subservient to a disposition in which enemies are approached as friends; and in which excess, and possibly even subsistence-level resources, are surrendered and sacrificed for the good, or love, of others.

Love in Luke 7:1–10—The Centurion

The next use of love occurs in the account of the centurion, a pericope adjacent to the Sermon on the Plain. For the first time, Luke attributes the description of love to a particular person. On the one hand, the centurion is a socially honorable figure by some, while considered tainted by others, and on the other hand, his slave is a member of the perceived inferior and neglected class. However, the slave is honored by the centurion's esteem as he dispatches Jewish community elders as brokers to summon Jesus's assistance.

Most curious is the Lukan contribution to this narrative, that these elders are not described as loving the centurion, but rather they describe the centurion as one who loves, *agapaos*, their nation (7:5). One might expect *phileo* to have been employed in such a patronage relationship, but this is no ordinary patron-client situation. This centurion, who is a gentile, and at that, a representative of controversial occupying powers, is nevertheless the first human individual attributed the quality of love by Luke (7:9). Interestingly, this follows shortly after Jesus's direction to love one's enemies; therefore, this centurion loves a nation that remains in considerable conflict with the powers the centurion represents.

This centurion is an exemplary Lukan character. Not only is he a gentile, but he is presented as being generous, having constructed a synagogue in Capernaum (7:5). The centurion is further characterized by his modesty: Even though he is of high, honorable status, he rightly sees himself as unworthy of Jesus entering his home (7:6). Humility is an exceptional Lukan temperament, and the fact that he sees himself as unworthy in comparison to a peasant, itinerant Jewish teacher is hallmark Lukan material.

At this point in the Gospel, Jesus had first been rejected in Nazareth (4:16–30). Then he has been resisted by lawyers and Pharisees following his healing of the paralytic and sharing table fellowship with suspect groups (5:12–32). Next, he has been rejected by scribes and Pharisees concerning his Sabbath ethic (6:1–11). Accordingly, the response of this centurion is not only unique, but it contrasts with the prior response of those who have rejected Jesus.

Luke depicts the centurion as a model of love through his relinquishing of status and monies and his recognition of Jesus. Accordingly, Jesus remarks that his faith is unique in all Israel, another vibrant component to his persona. This is the most robust receptivity of Jesus at this point in the gospel and is only later rivaled by Zacchaeus, another complex character in Luke 19.

CHAPTER 13: WHERE'S THE LOVE?

Love in Luke 7:36–50—The Woman Who Washed Jesus's Feet

Agapao and its derivatives appear three more times in the same chapter (7:42, 45), in the context of the parable of two debtors (7:41–43). This usage of love requires a bit of explanation to unpack as this parable elucidates the actions of the woman anointing Jesus's feet. Once more, the language is employed surrounding socio-economic and interpersonal relationships, and for the first time, the direct implication of this love is applied from humanity toward God.

Separated by just two pericopes from the centurion, once more an honorable type is featured, Simon the Pharisee, who hosts Jesus at his home. Interestingly and noticeably, the centurion, a model of faith attested by Jesus, had seen himself as unworthy for Jesus to be under his roof; however, evidently in contrast shortly thereafter, Simon, a Pharisee, who should be a most proper model of faith, does see himself fit to extend Jesus such an invitation.

Where Simon is further suspect is his lack of common hospitality—failing to offer Jesus a welcome kiss, water to wash his own feet, or oil to anoint his head (7:44–46). Juxtaposed with Simon is a woman with a dishonorable reputation. She complicates matters further through her culturally shameful, inappropriate actions, kissing Jesus's feet and wiping them with her hair (7:38).[5] To frame this simply and succinctly, at best, this is not something a woman would do for anyone other than the closest of kin, if even that. Moreover, the Jews of antiquity had such a stigma regarding this such that even those who became slaves retained their dignity by refusing to wash the feet of their master.[6] This woman would now be viewed as at least guilty of a double social faux pas, seeming to substantiate her unmeritorious reputation attested by Simon, the host.

However, Luke's audience is meant to grasp that Simon, while being socially honorable, is yet greedy by withholding hospitable gestures, and he is perhaps ungrateful, as demonstrated by the subsequent parable of the debtors. Meanwhile the anonymous woman, although woefully lower on the social scale, is the one shown to behave honorably, at least in theological terms, in that she has even lowered herself further by acting as lower than a slave, for the benefit of Jesus.

---

5. Malina and Rohrbaugh, *Social-Science Commentary on John*, 205.
6. Van der Watt, "Meaning of Jesus Washing," 25–40.

Love in Luke 7:36–50—Parable of the Two Debtors

The subsequent parable of the debtors injects a further socio-economic dynamic as well as the inclusion of the love paradigm. Simply put, two debts were forgiven, and naturally, the one forgiven of most debt *loves* the most. To consider the impact of this to Jesus's audience, first-century Jewish Palestine was burdened by a substantial debt problem leading to a massive loss of land to pay balances.[7] This led to a form of exile, of persons who had lost their ancestral homes and therefore their communities. Some even endured either themselves or their family members becoming debt slaves. The problem was so systemic that debt language became a quite effective surrogate for sin, which also caused the loss of ancestral land leading to exile throughout the Hebrew narrative.

While it would be a mistake to overemphasize the socio-economic implications of this parable and ignore the more fundamental forgiveness of sins, it is also detrimental to avoid the elements of debt release and other financial and material ethics asserted by Jesus and their thematic connection here. The generosity expressed in the Sermon on the Plain from the previous chapter, giving without expecting a return, has significant implications toward debt behavior.

The pericope with the parable of two debtors contains a story and setting that is also Lukan unique. Previously, the unlikely gentile centurion modeled love and faith to the Jewish elders; now, in this instance, the improbable, shameful woman illustrates love to the religious elitist, Simon the Pharisee. Herein is another example of status reversal, benefiting the marginalized, with the incorporation of economic implications.

Love in Luke 10:25–37—Parable of the Good Samaritan

The next deployment of *agapao* occurs in the narrative surrounding the parable of the ambiguously identified good Samaritan in Luke 10:30–35. The occasion of the parable is that of the questioning lawyer and his ultimate response quoting Deut 6:5 and Lev 19:18, to love God with all one's heart and faculties and one's neighbor as self. The prelude with the lawyer shares some precedent with the synoptic tradition; however, the proceeding example, the parable qualifying who one should love as well as the characteristics exemplifying love, is a Lukan-only contribution.

---

7. Wright, *Jesus and the Victory of God*, 380.

The story is open to multiple potential interpretations of the lawyer's questioning of Jesus. According to the most optimistic commentators' perspective, his question could be born out of ignorance, not understanding the components of applying *agapao* to God and neighbor. However, the lawyer is not presented as being ignorant but instead as divisive, engaging in an honor challenge with Jesus using love as a variable in his test. The most negative outlook would be that this lawyer is seeking to delimit his efforts of love. Some in first-century Judaism went as far as viewing themselves as exempt from having to show love to specific segments of their own Jewish population.[8] Regardless of the lawyer's intentions, assuredly, he is not the example of love.

In this selection, Luke again juxtaposes his characters. Those in religious categories include the lawyer, a status that Luke uses synonymously with that of Pharisees and scribes, versus Jesus; and the priest and Levite, who are aligned with bandits while contrasted with the Samaritan and innkeeper. The injection of the priest and Levite, characters with the most sacred posture on the purity map, along with their failed modeling of the commandment, is particularly compelling.

In the parable, an example story of love, the priest and the Levite occupy a posture parallel to the bandits on the road, retaining the highest degree of culpability as demonstrated by their inactivity.[9] As before, the expectation is that these characters should be best positioned to grasp the theological implications of love, like Simon the Pharisee and the inquisitive lawyer of Luke 10:25–37; however, they remain either woefully ignorant or perhaps unwilling to demonstrate love through action. Simon the Pharisee and the lawyer from Luke 10:25–37 presumably invest a considerable amount of time attempting to understand and perfect the implications of lawful behavior. Meanwhile, the vocational responsibilities of the temple agents in the parable are to serve in a mediatory role between God and humanity. However, those whose station places them in what should be nearest to theological truth nevertheless shamefully fail to grasp the approaching realities of God's kingdom. These characters represent the antithesis of Luke's ideal of love, which will be explored further.

In contrast with these poor examples who fail to properly display love, the character that Luke articulates as truly displaying love is once more an unlikely source. This time, it is not a gentile centurion, the representative

---

8. Bock, *Luke*, 2:1293.
9. Vinson, *Luke*.

of foreign occupation and empire who pollutes sacred soil; or a woman, of all people, with a shameful reputation who seems to socially validate her public dishonor at the dinner table. In this case it is an additionally suspect character, the anonymous Samaritan.

Jesus's immediate audience likely would have found the inclusion of the character of the Samaritan deeply unsettling. This was not only because of his ethnicity—quoting from John's Gospel, "the Jews have no dealings with Samaritans" (4:9)—but because one of the primary fears of a closed sub-society is the infiltration of polluted lineage. He would have been disturbing not merely because of the history between the Jews and Samaritans, which included profaned temple conduct and bloodshed, but also because he is traveling in sacred space between two critical political and religious locations, Jerusalem and Jericho. Worse, the Samaritan carried oil, wine, and money, indicating he may have been a merchant transacting business between these two key economic cities. He seems a person of some means, appearing to have excess, which was true only for the minority 10 percent of the populace in the Roman and Palestinian economies.[10] To a peasant audience, this would have been a signal to distrust this character, as those who were economically prosperous in a zero-sum economy tended to be exploitative.[11]

Despite all this, the Samaritan shows love by becoming a neighbor, acting like an insider while on outside soil, and by attaching himself to one who was vulnerable. He risks his own welfare, not only by exposing himself to the dangers of bandits on the road, but also through vulnerably toting a half-dead presumed Hebrew down the road in a world where Samaritans were prone to injustices. This story presents economic ethics not only through the Samaritan's sacrifice of expensive oil and wine in caring for the traveler, but also via his committal of a debt obligation to an innkeeper, whose vocation was considered disreputable and exploitative. The process of love includes not only the forgiveness of others' debts, but the vulnerability of entering debt obligations on behalf of humanity.

Positive Relational Love in Acts

The impact of the material ethics including giving without expectation, debt forgiveness, and other financial ethics asserted by Jesus, in terms of

10. Friesen, "Injustice or God's Will?," 19–20.
11. Van Eck, "Samaritan Merchant," 5.

this chapter, is their connection to the theme of love. Jesus's thesis in the parable of the woman who washed his feet in Luke 7 is that the forgiveness of sins and debts enable one to return love and attachment back to God. Thus, the woman who washed Jesus's feet unquestionably showed love. This also seems to be the author's intent regarding the early *ecclesia* in Acts. This community lived out Jesus's ethics in a setting in which all things were in common, and everyone's needs were cared for, to the extent that property was relinquished for the community good.

This is the second case in which love is evidenced in Acts. Rather than replicating a patronage model of society, the early church incorporated the structure and ethic of a kin group.[12] Naturally, being in a family would imply, if not demand, love, not merely in terms of affection, but as an attachment. Therefore, although the word *love* is not used in Acts, the action of love is shown among the early Christ community in such a way. This love was not only enabled by the power of the Holy Spirit attachment but was also made functional by the same Spirit. Luke chapter 3 signifies a momentous occasion in the development of Jesus's character in relation to the Father. Simply put, the moment of Jesus's baptism and Holy Spirit reception is where Sonship is most authoritatively attested. Accordingly, the testimony in Acts of baptism and Holy Spirit reception along with the kin group behavior more than adequately demonstrates that the early church saw these experiences as bringing them into a kinship posture with the Father, through Christ. Therefore, love is articulated in Acts through the incorporation of a kin group.

Negative Relational Love

The remaining occurrences of the word *love* in his Gospel represent the antithesis of the right kind of love. The understanding of love as having a primary relational component in collectivistic societies becomes a pertinent bridge to Luke 16:9 where Jesus warns of making *philos* ("friends") with unjust money. Here, the idea of attachment, in the form of friendship, or perhaps even a patronage relationship, with the unjust, or with money itself, becomes a concern. Four verses later, Jesus asserts that no one can serve two masters, otherwise they will hate one while *agapesie* ("loving") the other. The Pharisees, however, in the following verse (14) are said to be *philargyoi* ("lovers of, or those attached to") money.

12. DeSilva, *Honor, Patronage, Kinship and Purity*, 200.

In Luke, these Pharisees' attachment to, or love of, money and status is well attested. In 20:46, in Jerusalem, Jesus warns of the scribes who *phileo* to be greeted with honor among the crowds. In Luke 11:42, the Pharisees tithe well, but disregard *agapene*. In the following verse 43, they *agapate* the honorable community seats. These Pharisees, lawyers, and scribes (identities that Luke uses interchangeably) place burdens on the populace they serve (11:46). They resist the Jesus movement as well as having opposed John the Baptizer. One critical component of the kingdom they resist is the great reversal because of their love for wealth and status.

This negative use of the word *love* in connection with Lukan economic ethic and reversal bears further exploration. These antagonists oppose Jesus's Sabbath ethics in Luke 6:1–11 and 14:1–6. However, while ostensibly protecting the Sabbath, they are rejecting reversal. In Jesus's practice of true Sabbath as his disciples plucked the grain of corn, it is understood that the hungry cannot enjoy Sabbath rest until they are fed, echoing Jesus's words, "Blessed are the hungry" (Luke 6:21). In the case of Jesus's Sabbath healing, those who are plagued with serious physical infirmities cannot receive true Sabbath rest without proper care.

The same group is reported to oppose open table fellowship, specifically with tax collectors and sinners, in Luke 5:27–32 and 15:1–2. The former account produces the parable asserting that new wine must be poured into new wineskins (Luke 5:33–39). Simply put, the old template is insufficient.

Then, in Luke 15:1–2, in response to the Pharisees' dissatisfaction with Jesus's ethics, Jesus offers three parables climaxing with that of the so-called prodigal son (Luke 15:3–32). Although the latter contains certain nuances, it is well understood that the father of this parable corresponds to God or even to Jesus. The younger brother portrays the exiles that Jesus is collecting, while the elder brother symbolizes those who refuse fellowship, including the Pharisees among others.

This parable of the prodigal son is often seen as a prime example of forgiveness and reconciliation, as well it should be. However, the economic ethics that are pertinent to the story should not be neglected, as they illustrate Luke's purpose. Most compellingly, the father is willing to continue to sacrifice wealth, possessions, and honor to reattach to or love his son; meanwhile, the elder brother is presented as greedy, turning the fatted calf into a surrogate for his frustrations and as an excuse for selfishness. In his protest of the father's material ethics, he voluntarily removes himself from the status of a son to that of slave and becomes an exile. This parable, among other things, attests to the adage "look what the negative use of money can do to a family."

Jesus is building a community out of a reversal. Therefore, those with the most honor and wealth to protect naturally become the most threatened, including the lawyers, scribes, and Pharisees, who embody the antithesis of love in the Lukan text.

Findings on Love in Luke-Acts

To reiterate the findings of this study, first, Luke attests love to be extended from the Father to the Son, evidenced by the Holy Spirit dispatch and the bookends of *agapao* in Luke 3 and 20. This Holy Spirit attachment is also useful in constructing love as a relational quality extended from the Father to the *ecclesia* in Acts.

The most quantitative theme of love in this Gospel is expressed in context with models of socio-economic expectancy within Jesus's proclamation of the kingdom of God. The benefits of these ethics generate a love for or attachment to God, most specifically connected to the forgiveness of sins. Additionally, and presented most robustly, the granting of this reversal enables one to reproduce these ethics within the community.

Luke identifies both a holy love as well as a profane love that incorporates interpersonal relationships. On the sacred end of the spectrum is a love that produces humility, the self-surrender of social status when needed, and a sacrifice of money and possessions, particularly for the benefit of others. In this way, love is never presented as being void of the tangible social effects being demonstrated through one's actions.

In contrast, polluted love, as articulated by Luke, is marked by selfish components, and it is attached to the esteem of status and wealth, especially to the extent that these receive more weight than other needful qualities. Admittedly, this is not a complex proposition; however, it remains vital to identify this as a particular theological understanding in the Lukan corpus. As much as love is remarked upon in modern Christian circles, particularly the relational aspect of God's love for humanity, the Lukan Jesus indicates that this love should not be divorced from socio-economic ethics, but rather should be dependent upon them.

The theme of love in Luke-Acts and its connection to Lukan economic ethics represents a significant gap in terms of broader scholarship. However, this creates a substantial opportunity for interaction and dialogue by Lukan scholarship on the topics covered in this chapter, as well as occurrences of love outside the direct lexical context.

Bibliography

Bailey, Kenneth E. *Finding the Lost: Cultural Keys to Luke 15*. St. Louis, MO: Concordia, 1992.
Balz, Horst Robert, and Gerhard Schneider. *Exegetical Dictionary of the New Testament*. 3 vols. Grand Rapids, MI: Eerdmans, 1990–1993.
Barclay, John M. G. *Paul and the Gift*. Grand Rapids, MI: Eerdmans, 2015.
———. "Paul and the Gift." Webinar, Hindustan Bible Institute, November 23, 2023.
———. *Paul and the Power of Grace*. Grand Rapids, MI: Eerdmans, 2020.
Bates, Matthew W. *Gospel Allegiance: What Faith in Jesus Misses for Salvation in Christ*. Ada, MI: Brazos, 2019.
———. *Salvation by Allegiance Alone: Rethinking Faith, Works, and the Gospel of Jesus the King*. Ada, MI: Baker Academic, 2017.
Berding, Kenneth. "The Hermeneutical Framework of Social-Scientific Criticism: How Much Can Evangelicals Get Involved?" *The Evangelical Quarterly* 75.1 (Jan–Mar 2003) 3–22.
Bock, Darrell L. *Luke*. 2 vols. Baker Exegetical Commentary on the New Testament. Reprint, Ada, MI: Baker Academic, 2016. Kindle ed.
———. *A Theology of Luke and Acts: God's Promised Program, Realized for All Nations*. Biblical Theology of the New Testament Series. Edited by A. J. Köstenberger. Grand Rapids, MI: Zondervan, 2015. Kindle ed.
Borg, Marcus, and John Dominic Crossan. *The First Christmas: What the Gospels Really Teach about Jesus's Birth*. New York: HarperCollins, 2007.
Bruce, F. F. *The Book of the Acts*. Grand Rapids, MI: Eerdmans, 1988.
Charlesworth, James H. *Jesus and Temple: Textual and Archaeological Explorations*. Minneapolis: Fortress, 2014. Kindle ed.
Chen, Diane G. *Luke*. New Covenant Commentary Series. Eugene, OR: Cascade, 2017. Kindle ed.
Conzelmann, Hans. *Acts of the Apostles*. Hermeneia: A Critical and Historical Commentary on the Bible. Minneapolis: Fortress, 1988.
Conzelmann, Hans, and Walther Zimmerli. *Theological Dictionary of the New Testament*. Edited by Gerhard Kittel et al. Grand Rapids, MI: Eerdmans, 1964.
Crossan, John Dominic. "Roman Imperial Theology." In *In the Shadow of Empire: Reclaiming the Bible as a History of Faithful Resistance*, edited by Richard A. Horsley, 59–74. Louisville, KY: Westminster John Knox, 2008.

BIBLIOGRAPHY

deSilva, David A. *Honor, Patronage, Kinship and Purity: Unlocking New Testament Culture.* Downers Grove, IL: InterVarsity, 2012.

Dewey, Joanna. "The Literacy Structure of the Controversy Stories in Mark 2:1—3:6." *Journal of Biblical Literature* 92.3 (1973) 394–401.

Douglas, Mary. *Purity and Danger: An Analysis of the Concepts of Pollution and Taboo.* New York: Routledge and Kegan Paul, 1966.

Dunn, James D. G. "Baptism in the Holy Spirit: Yet One More—Again." *Journal of Pentecostal Theology* 19 (2010).

Dvorak, James D. "John H. Elliott's Social-Scientific Criticism." *Trinity Journal* 28.2 (Fall 2007) 251–78.

Edwards, James R. *The Gospel according to Luke.* Pillar New Testament Commentary. Edited by D. A. Carson. Grand Rapids, MI: Eerdmans, 2015. Kindle ed.

Elliott, John H. *A Home for the Homeless.* Philadelphia: Fortress, 1981.

———. *What Is Social-Scientific Criticism?* Edited by Dan O. Via Jr. Minneapolis: Fortress, 1993.

Fee, Gordon D. *New Testament Exegesis.* 3rd ed. Louisville, KY: Westminster John Knox, 2002. Kindle ed.

Fee, Gordon D., and Douglas Stuart. *How to Read the Bible for All Its Worth.* 3rd ed. Grand Rapids, MI: Zondervan, 2003.

Fiensy, David A. *The Social History of Palestine in the Herodian Period: The Land Is Mine.* Studies in the Bible and Early Christianity 20. Lewiston, NY: Mellen, 1991.

Fiensy, David A., and Ralph K. Hawkins. *The Galilean Economy in the Time of Jesus.* Early Christianity and Its Literature. Atlanta: Society of Biblical Literature, 2013.

Fitzmyer, Joseph A. *The Acts of the Apostles: A New Translation with Introduction and Commentary.* The Anchor Bible 31: Acts. New Haven, CT: Yale University Press, 2008.

———. *The Gospel according to Luke I–IX: Introduction, Translation, and Notes.* Anchor Yale Bible Commentaries 28A. New York: Doubleday, 1982.

Friesen, S. J. "Injustice or God's Will? Early Christian Explanations of Poverty." In *Wealth and Poverty in Early Church and Society: Holy Cross Studies in Patristic Theology and History*, edited by Susan R. Holman. Grand Rapids, MI: Baker Academic, 2008.

Goodman, Martin. "Chapter 5: The Pilgrimage Economy of Jerusalem in the Second Temple Period." In *Judaism and the Roman World: Collected Essays.* Ancient Judaism and Early Christianity. Leiden: Brill, 2006.

Green, Joel B. *The Gospel of Luke.* The New International Commentary on the New Testament. Grand Rapids, MI: Eerdmans, 1997. Kindle ed.

Hays, Christopher M. *Luke's Wealth Ethics: A Study in Their Coherence and Character.* Tübingen: Mohr Siebeck, 2010.

Hays, J. Daniel. *The Temple and the Tabernacle: A Study of God's Dwelling Places from Genesis to Revelation.* Grand Rapids, MI: Baker, 2016. Kindle ed.

Heen, Erik. "Radical Patronage in Luke-Acts." *Currents in Theology and Mission* 33.6 (2006) 445–58.

Herzog, William R., II. *Jesus, Justice and the Reign of God: A Ministry of Liberation.* Louisville, KY: Westminster John Knox, 2000.

Hill, David. *New Testament Prophecy.* New Foundations Theological Library. Atlanta: John Knox, 1979.

Horsley, Richard A. *Jesus and Empire: The Kingdom of God and the New World Disorder.* Minneapolis: Fortress, 2003. Kindle ed.

BIBLIOGRAPHY

———. *Jesus and the Powers: Conflict, Covenant, and the Hope of the Poor*. Minneapolis: Fortress, 2011. Kindle ed.

Johnson, Luke Timothy. *The Acts of the Apostles*. Sacra Pagina 5. Edited by Daniel J. Harrington. Collegeville, MN: Liturgical, 1992.

———. *The Gospel of Luke*. Sacra Pagina. Collegeville, MN: Liturgical, 1991.

Just Arthur A., Jr., *Luke 1:1—9:50*. Concordia Commentary. St. Louis, MO: Concordia, 1996.

Keener, Craig S. *Acts: An Exegetical Commentary*. Vol. 3, *15:1—23:35*. Grand Rapids, MI: Baker Academic, 2014.

———. *Acts: An Exegetical Commentary*. Vol. 2, *3:1—14:28*. Ada, MI: Baker Academic, 2013.

———. *The Gospel of Matthew: A Socio-Rhetorical Commentary*. Grand Rapids, MI: Eerdmans, 1999. Kindle ed.

———. *The IVP Bible Background Commentary: New Testament*. Downers Grove, IL: InterVarsity, 2014.

———. *The Spirit in the Gospels and Acts: Divine Purity and Power*. Grand Rapids, MI: Baker Academic, 2010.

Larkin, William J., Jr. *Acts*. The IVP New Testament Commentary Series. Downers Grove, IL: InterVarsity, 1995.

Louw, Johannes P., and Eugene Albert Nida. *Greek-English Lexicon of the New Testament: Based on Semantic Domains*. New York: United Bible Societies, 1996.

Malina, Bruce J. "Grace/Favor." In *Handbook of Biblical Social Values*, 3rd ed., Matrix: The Bible in Mediterranean Context 10, edited by John J. Pilch and Bruce J. Malina, 75–77. Eugene, OR: Cascade, 2016.

Malina, Bruce J., and Richard L. Rohrbaugh. *Social-Science Commentary on the Gospel of John*. Minneapolis: Fortress, 1998.

Marcus, Joel. *Mark 1–8: A New Translation with Introduction and Commentary*. Anchor Yale Bible 27. New Haven, CT: Yale University Press, 2008.

Marshall, I. Howard. *Acts: An Introduction and Commentary*. Tyndale New Testament Commentaries 5. Downers Grove, IL: InterVarsity, 1980.

Mathew, Sam P. *Temple-Criticism in Mark's Gospel: The Economic Role of the Jerusalem Temple during the First Century CE*. Delhi: Indian Society for Promoting Christian Knowledge, 1999.

McCown, C. C. "Geography of Palestine." In *The Interpreter's Dictionary of the Bible, An Illustrated Encyclopedia in Four Volumes*. Vol. 3, *K–Q*, edited by George Arthur Buttrick, 626–39. Nashville: Abingdon, 1962.

McHugh, John. *The Mother of Jesus in the New Testament*. New York: Doubleday, 1975.

Miller, Amanda C. "Cut from the Same Cloth: A Study of Female Patrons in Luke-Acts and the Roman Empire." *Review and Expositor* 114.2 (2017) 203–10.

Montanari, Franco. *The Brill Dictionary of Ancient Greek*. Edited by Madeleine Goh and Chad Schroeder. Leiden: Brill, 2015.

Montero, Roman A. *All Things in Common: The Economic Practices of the Early Christians*. Eugene, OR: Wipf & Stock, 2017. Kindle ed.

Moxnes, Halvor. "Patron-Client Relations and the New Community of Luke-Acts." In *The Social World of Luke-Acts*, edited by Jerome H. Neyrey, 241–68. Peabody, MA: Hendrickson, 1991.

BIBLIOGRAPHY

Neyrey, Jerome. "The Idea of Purity in Mark in Social Scientific Criticism of the New Testament and Its World." In *Social-Scientific Criticism of the New Testament and Its Social World*. Semeia Studies 35, edited by John H. Elliott, 95–96. Atlanta: Scholars, 1986.

———. "Limited Good." In *Handbook of Biblical Social Values*, 3rd ed., Matrix: The Bible in Mediterranean Context 10, edited by John J. Pilch and Bruce J. Malina, 103–6. Eugene, OR: Cascade, 2016.

Niehoff, Maren R. "Circumcision as a Marker of Identity: Philo, Origen and the Rabbis on Gen 17: 1—14." *Jewish Studies Quarterly* 10.2 (2003) 89–123.

Oakman, Douglas E. *The Political Aims of Jesus*. Minneapolis: Fortress, 2012. Kindle ed.

Pilch, John J. *A Cultural Handbook to the Bible*. Grand Rapids, MI: Eerdmans, 2012. Kindle ed.

Pilch, John J., and Bruce J. Malina. *Handbook of Biblical Social Values*. 3rd ed. Matrix: The Bible in Mediterranean Context 10. Eugene, OR: Cascade, 2016. Kindle ed.

Reese, James, and John Pilch. "Love." In *Handbook of Biblical Social Values*, 3rd ed., Matrix: The Bible in Mediterranean Context 10, edited by John J. Pilch and Bruce J. Malina, 106–9. Eugene, OR: Cascade, 2016.

Reumann, John. *Philippians: A New Translation with Introduction and Commentary*. Anchor Yale Bible Commentaries 33B. New Haven, CT: Yale University Press, 2008.

Richards, E. R., and R. James. *Misreading Scripture with Individualist Eyes: Patronage, Honor, and Shame in the Biblical World*. Downers Grove, IL: IVP Academic, 2020.

Rohrbaugh, Richard L. "Honor and Shame: Core Values of the Biblical World." DVD lecture. Washington, DC: Biblical Archaeology Society, 2001.

———. *The New Testament in Cross-Cultural Perspective*. Matrix: The Bible in Mediterranean Context 1. Eugene, OR: Cascade, 2017.

———. "Peasants, Widows, Bandits and Beggars: The Everyday World in Which Jesus Lived." DVD lecture. Washington, DC: Biblical Archaeology Society, 2009.

———, ed. *The Social Sciences and New Testament Interpretation*. Peabody, MA: Hendrickson, 1996.

Sanders, E. P. *Jesus and Judaism*. Philadelphia: Fortress, 1985. Kindle ed.

Shinall, Myrick C., Jr. "The Social Condition of Lepers in the Gospels." *Journal of Biblical Literature* 137.4 (Dec 2018) 915–34.

Silva, M., ed. *New International Dictionary of New Testament Theology and Exegesis*. 2nd ed. Grand Rapids, MI: Zondervan, 2014.

Smith, Mitzi. "Acts." In *Lexham Context Commentary: New Testament*, edited by D. Mangum. Bellingham, WA: Lexham, 2020.

Spicq, Ceslas, and James D. Ernest. *Theological Lexicon of the New Testament*. Peabody, MA: Hendrickson, 2014.

VanderKam, James C. *From Joshua to Caiaphas: High Priests after the Exile*. Philadelphia: Fortress, 2004. Kindle ed.

van der Watt, Jan. "The Meaning of Jesus Washing the Feet of His Disciples (John 13)." *Neotestamentica* 51.1 (2017) 25–40.

van Eck, Ernest. "A Samaritan Merchant and His Friend, and Their Friends: Practicing Life-Giving Theology." *HTS Theological Studies* 75.1 (2019).

Vinson, Richard B. *Luke*. Smyth and Helwys Bible Commentary. Macon, GA: Smyth and Helwys, 2008.

Wall, Robert W. "Successors to 'the Twelve' according to Acts 12:1–17." *The Catholic Biblical Quarterly* 53.4 (991) 628–43.

BIBLIOGRAPHY

Wright, N. T. *The Day the Revolution Began: Reconsidering the Meaning of Jesus's Crucifixion*. New York: HarperOne, 2016. Kindle ed.
———. *Jesus and the Victory of God*. Christian Origins and the Question of God 2. Minneapolis: Fortress, 1997. Kindle ed.
———. *The New Testament and the People of God*. Christian Origins and the Question of God 1. Minneapolis: Augsburg Fortress, 1992. Kindle ed.
Wright, N. T., and Michael F. Bird. *The New Testament in Its World: An Introduction to the History, Literature, and Theology of the First Christians*. Grand Rapids, MI: Zondervan Academic, 2019.

www.ingramcontent.com/pod-product-compliance
Lightning Source LLC
Chambersburg PA
CBHW050804160426
43192CB00010B/1643